Your StrengthsQuest access code is

X5X3D6R3F2C8E7

The Web address is

www.strengthsquest.com

(Code valid for one user only)

E-mail: _____

User name: _____

Password: _____

StrengthsQuest:

DISCOVER AND DEVELOP YOUR
STRENGTHS IN ACADEMICS,
CAREER, AND BEYOND

Donald O. Clifton, Ph.D. &
Edward "Chip" Anderson, Ph.D.
with Laurie A. Schreiner, Ph.D.

New York

GALLUP PRESS
1251 Avenue of the Americas
23rd Floor
New York, NY 10020

Cover design by Chin-Yee Lai

First edition 2002
Second edition 2006

17

ISBN 10: 1-59562-011-7
ISBN 13: 978-1-59562-011-8

to those who helped me discover my strengths:
my wife Shirley, and our family

—DON

to God, my Creator, who inspired this work, gave me talents to do this
work, and guided me to my beloved wife, Irma

—CHIP

to my daughter Lindsey, who is becoming the person she was created to be,
and to my parents, who always affirmed my God-given talents

—LAURIE

Note to Educators

The second edition of *StrengthsQuest: Discover and Develop Your Strengths in Academics, Career, and Beyond* is an attempt to be responsive to student needs while preserving the voice and vision of the original authors, Chip Anderson and Don Clifton. Don passed away in October of 2003 and Chip died in July of 2005. Both men had great passion for students. Both were giants in the movement to bring a strengths "revolution" to higher education.

More than 100,000 copies of the first edition of the StrengthsQuest book were sold since its publication in 2002. The book introduced tens of thousands of college students, their families, and the faculty and staff who worked with them to a major paradigm shift in higher education: to see students as bringing innate talents with them into the college environment — talents that, when combined with skills and knowledge in strengths development, would lead to their achievement and success. *Build on great talents rather than focus on deficit remediation* was Don and Chip's exhortation as they traveled across the country. They were determined to see a strengths revolution — and they certainly planted the seeds of that revolution through their powerful presence.

As Chip's friend and colleague, I still hear his inspirational voice while writing this edition: "What would we do if we really loved our students?" Those words have given me direction in writing, and the result is my answer to that question. If we really love our students, we will ensure that each one knows how uniquely talented he or she is. We will see and nurture the potential in them. We will care deeply about the meanings and purposes of their lives and we will help them see the connections between their powerful talents and their callings and their futures. We will focus on helping them build strong, healthy relationships as the foundation for a satisfying life. And we will give them practical suggestions for how to do all of this.

This new edition is also an important step in continuing Don and Chip's legacies. With their deaths, many of us wondered what would become of the strengths movement. But Connectedness was an area of powerful talent in Chip; he saw everything he did in life as part of a Master plan. He knew that his actions would have a ripple effect long after he was gone. He knew there was a reason our paths crossed. So this edition is my best effort to honor his life and work, and to be part of the "ripple effect" in higher education.

New features you'll find in this edition include:

- Fresh student voices and action items (Chapter 3, "Affirming and Celebrating Your Talents")

- New material on relationships (Chapter 4, "Relationships from the Strengths Perspective")

- New suggestions for making the most of your talents in each theme (Chapter 5, "Insights Into Strengths Development")

- A new approach to the career chapters, based on research we've done with college students and the Holland vocational types.

- A new appendix with detail on the relationship between Signature Themes and the Holland types, based on the national validity study of the Clifton StrengthsFinder with college students.

You'll also find a wealth of resources available to instructors on the StrengthsQuest Web site at www.strengthsquest.com. Please take advantage of the material that is available to assist you with class activities and assignments.

I hope you'll find this edition provides your students with a new look at how identifying their most naturally powerful talents and building upon them to create strengths can be the first step toward becoming the persons they were created to be — and experiencing success in college, career, and beyond!

—Laurie A. Schreiner

Table of Contents

StrengthsQuest:

DISCOVER AND DEVELOP YOUR
STRENGTHS IN ACADEMICS,
CAREER, AND BEYOND

Preface

I was wrong!

For nearly half of my professional career, I was wrong about how to help students achieve. I had the wrong focus, made inaccurate assumptions, used faulty logic, and came to the wrong conclusions about how to increase student achievement.

During almost 36 years as a college administrator and instructor, I designed programs and services, taught classes, and conducted workshops with one purpose in mind: To help students gain maximum benefits from college and continue achieving long after they are done with school.

Looking back, however, I now see that for the first 15 years, despite my best intentions, I was using the wrong approach. About the only thing I did right during those early years was to invest myself in students, express my care and concern for them as people, and encourage them. But although a high percentage of my students persisted in and graduated from the programs in which I worked, they seldom became top achievers, and few achieved to levels of excellence.

Here is where and how I went wrong: I had read the research reports that clearly indicated a correlation between academic preparation and achievement. Results from almost every study on students in high school and college showed a direct correlation between students' levels of academic preparation and their subsequent achievement and persistence in college. The statistics showed that students who had the best academic preparation earned the highest grades and persisted to graduation in larger numbers. Students who had the weakest academic preparation earned the lowest grades and had the lowest graduation rates.

Armed with this information, I began designing procedures to identify the students who were least prepared so that we could build programs and services that would help more students achieve. I assumed that there were certain preparation levels that students needed in order to accomplish more in school; that if students met or exceeded these preparation levels, everything would take care of itself; that if students were prepared and met the expectations of the professors, then the normal courses of study and interactions with faculty would be sufficient to help students develop and achieve.

But I began to see two potential problems with my assumptions.

1. Many students don't have the expected level of preparation.

2. The whole issue of preparation is complex, because there are so many different ways to prepare students to attain academic excellence.

After interviewing hundreds of students who were dropping out, experiencing difficulties, or flunking out of college, I came to believe that the types of preparation students needed included three broad areas: academic skills, background knowledge, and self-management skills. Within each of these areas, there were several specific types of skills and knowledge that instructors expected.

Assuming that certain skills and knowledge were the foundation of student success, I organized various diagnostic, testing, and assessment procedures to determine the extent to which each student was prepared in various areas. Diagnostic and assessment areas included: reading speed and comprehension; vocabulary level; knowledge of mathematical concepts and problem-solving; knowledge of grammar and writing skills; knowledge and problem-solving in chemistry and physics; knowledge of study skills and study attitudes; and time and stress management. Using a combination of standardized tests, institutionally developed instruments, and interview procedures, I tried to get a clear picture of whether each student was prepared or underprepared.

In fact, I was very much influenced by the Deficit Remediation Educational Model, which has been predominant in education for decades. This model assumes that the most important thing to do is to "fix" the student. Programs and services based on this model are dedicated to helping students achieve by first diagnosing student needs, problems, ignorance, concerns, defects, and deficits. Those who use the Deficit Remediation Educational Model have the challenge of designing classes, workshops, programs, and services to help students improve in areas where they are underprepared. Based on the diagnosis, participation in remedial programs and services is often required. Students are usually prevented from pursuing other areas of study and from focusing on their interests until their "deficits" have been removed and their "problems" have been overcome.

Using this approach, students are usually told that they must overcome their deficiencies by a specific time. If they're unable to do so by the established date, students are usually dismissed or told that they aren't "college material." Mea culpa. I designed and implemented educational programs and services based on this model for almost 15 years, with the best of intentions. In retrospect, it's crystal clear that I was actually *preventing* students from becoming top achievers.

The Conference That Changed My Life

In the winter of 1978, I attended a conference on college-student retention, sponsored by American College Testing (ACT), which brought together some of the best researchers and practitioners in this field. The conference coordinators were Drs. Lee Noel and Randi Levitz, who later founded the largest consulting organization in college student recruitment and retention, Noel-Levitz Inc.

Drs. Noel and Levitz gave presentations on why nearly half of the students who go to college drop out or flunk out along the way. They presented research findings and described some of the most effective programs and services designed to help more students persist to graduation. Another presenter at this conference was Dr. Robert Cope, coauthor of the book *Revolving College Doors*. He presented the best theory and research available about the causes of student persistence and attrition.

From the combination of presentations by Drs. Noel, Levitz, and Cope, I was forced to come to a radically new conclusion about college-student success:

More students leave college because of disillusionment, discouragement, or reduced motivation than because of lack of ability or dismissal by school administration.

It's difficult to describe how mind-boggling this new conclusion was for me. I discovered that I had been wrong both in my logic and in the way I designed programs and services. Before the conference, I had concluded that students were leaving college because they lacked certain skills, knowledge, and abilities. All the work I had done was based on this premise.

With the dawning awareness that I had been operating from a faulty perspective, I was eventually forced to an even more devastating conclusion:

The deficit-based, remediation programming I had used for more than 10 years interfered *with students becoming top achievers.*

As I make these confessions, I feel bad about what I did unwittingly. I hindered students from achieving to levels of excellence.

But I wasn't alone. The deficit-based remediation approach was widely embraced by educators — and, unfortunately, remains the most prevalent approach used today. While most educators claim to identify not only the weaknesses but also the talents and strengths of their students, in practice, most focus almost solely on the weaknesses. Many students become demoralized and disillusioned.

The Impact of Meeting Donald O. Clifton

At the same conference in San Francisco, I met the man I feel so honored to know and write this book with: my coauthor, Dr. Donald O. Clifton. Don was introduced as a former professor at the University of Nebraska who had been voted Most Outstanding Educator for the state of Nebraska. Don had gone on to form a company called Selection Research, Incorporated, which helped companies do a better job of selecting employees through studying the "best of the best" in particular roles and positions. He eventually became chairman of The Gallup Organization, the global management consulting, training, and polling company.

I will never forget how Don slowly walked to the front of the stage, turned to the audience, and quickly had us riveted. His presentation drove home a significant point:

To produce excellence, you must study excellence.

Don's point hit me hard. Once again, I was wrong! In my efforts to help students persist and achieve, I had been studying dropouts. I should have been studying achievers! But back then, it seemed reasonable that to increase student persistence, I needed to study why students were leaving school and flunking out. Likewise, it seemed reasonable that to improve student achievement, I needed to study why people didn't achieve — which is why I spent endless hours interviewing dropouts and students who were underachieving.

It never occurred to me that I might be studying the wrong students to produce the best insights on how to help students achieve to levels of excellence. When I returned to UCLA after the conference in San Francisco, I began reading and trying to understand what made top achievers tick. Time and time again, I found that I had made inaccurate assumptions about the differences between top achievers and low achievers.

For example, I had always assumed that top achievers set high goals, and low achievers set low goals. But research indicates that top achievers tend to set goals *slightly above* their current level of performance, whereas low achievers often set very, very high goals.

The combination of reading books and articles, sitting in on classes attending workshops, and consulting with scholars in the field reinforced Don's contention that if you want to produce excellence, you have to study excellence.

Here is the most important insight I have gained from investigating excellence among college students: Top achievers aren't all alike. There are huge variations in how they approach learning and studying. Some seem to learn best in isolation, while others learn best in social settings. Some learn best through group discussions, while others learn best from self-testing and repetition. There isn't any "one size fits all" set of learning and study techniques. Top achievers capitalize on their own personal uniqueness as they learn.

Essentially, top achievers build their academic and personal lives — and later their careers — on their talents. They use those talents as the foundation of strengths development, and they apply those strengths to produce excellence. They also manage any weaknesses — lesser talents, skill, or knowledge that can detract from their performance or that of others. This is the same approach that Don Clifton has always advocated, and its effectiveness is supported by decades of Gallup research.

This book and the strengths approach to achieving in academics, career, and beyond represent a revolutionary departure from traditional and counterproductive philosophies and practices. We hope that its principles resonate with you, and that you apply the strengths approach to achieving success in all of your life's endeavors!

—Edward "Chip" Anderson

Chapter I

THE NATURE OF STRENGTHS

IMPORTANT

Your ID code is located on the first page of this book. Before you begin to read this book, it is essential that you use your ID code to log on to the StrengthsQuest Web site and take the Clifton StrengthsFinder assessment.

Go to:

www.strengthsquest.com

Minimum system requirements for the StrengthsQuest Web site:

- 33.6K modem (56K modem or faster recommended)
- Internet Explorer 5.5+ or Firefox 1.0+

Begin the StrengthsQuest program by taking the Clifton StrengthsFinder.

The Clifton StrengthsFinder is a 30-minute, Web-based assessment that measures the presence of talent in 34 areas called "themes." Immediately after you complete the assessment, a personalized Web site will be customized to your top five themes. Taking StrengthsFinder is a key starting point for your use of this book and the other StrengthsQuest components.

To purchase additional ID codes for the StrengthsQuest program, please visit www.strengthsquest.com/schoolaccess

At the 1996 Olympic Games in Atlanta, Kerri Strug was a gymnast on the United States women's gold-medal team. Her performance on the vault, as she nursed an injured ankle, remains one of the most memorable in Olympic history.

With 32,000 people in the Georgia Dome and millions watching her on television, Kerri fell on her first attempt at her most difficult twisting vault, severely spraining her left ankle. With less than a minute between vaults, and in great pain, she again attempted the vault, further injuring her ankle — but this time successfully landing on both feet. So she stood erect on one foot, raising both hands to salute the judges, then collapsed to her knees.

The crowd went wild. Kerri's vault earned a 9.712, and the U.S. women won the gold medal.

During that same year, Kerri was a freshman at UCLA. One of her classes required a research paper similar to a mini-doctoral dissertation. Students had to formulate their own research question and develop a questionnaire that was consistent with their research question. Then, the students would administer the questionnaire, collect and analyze the data, draw conclusions, and write a report that described the process. The written report was to be 35-40 pages long.

Taking the Clifton StrengthsFinder assessment was one of the class requirements. When Kerri took it, she scored extremely high in the Focus theme. But doesn't that make sense? Who else but a person with tremendous Focus talents could concentrate on completing her most difficult vault on an injured ankle in front of 32,000 screaming fans while Olympic gold hung in the balance? Who else could block out all of those distractions and then land on one foot without falling?

While Kerri certainly had other talents that enabled her to succeed, her Focus talents played a critical role. Without them, she might never have enjoyed such stunning Olympic success.

But there's more to the story. Toward the end of the fall term, as research papers were coming due, Kerri turned her paper in three days early, before any of the other 300-plus UCLA students in the class. She did this while traveling nearly every weekend on a national tour with fellow Olympic medalists. Even more remarkable was the way that Kerri could go out on an arena floor, do a routine, and then go underneath the stands and work on the paper. She would then go back out on the floor and do another routine and return to do more homework.

You see, Kerri also applied her Focus talents to succeed in academics.

Kerri is a remarkable young woman. But the excellence she achieved wasn't due simply to the fact that she naturally possessed talents. She recognized her Focus talents and built on them by adding skills and knowledge to create strength — the ability to produce consistent, near-perfect performance. She obviously did so at the Olympics — even while in severe pain and under tremendous pressure — but she was also able to apply her Focus in academics, where she achieved despite rigorous assignments and the myriad pressures of her athletic career.

Kerri has presented each of us with more than a shared pride in her Olympic success. We can learn from her. You, too, have talents. And in those talents you have the ability to meet challenges and achieve just as surely as Kerri did.

The Basics of Strengths

Talent: The Beginning of Strength

What is a strength? That's a good question, but strength begins with talent, so let's start there. A talent is a naturally recurring pattern of thought, feeling, or behavior that can be productively applied. A great number of talents naturally exist within you, and each of them is very specific. They are among the most real and most authentic aspects of your personhood. Your specific set of talents is a major part of what makes you a unique person, and that uniqueness holds great value for you and those around you. And your talents work in various combinations each time you do something very well, in your own unique way.

There is a direct connection between your talents and your achievements. Your talents empower you. They make it possible for you to move to higher levels of excellence and fulfill your potential. This is why it is so important for you to know, understand, and value your talents.

A talent represents a capacity to *do* something. In fact, when you are able to do something very well, you can be sure that at least one of your talents is involved. Just think about all the things you do very well. You'll realize that you have many talents!

And talents help you do something well not just once; they help you do it well over and over again. Because talents are naturally recurring patterns, they are "automatic," almost like breathing, so they repeatedly help you achieve.

That's not all, either. Each of your many talents can enable you to do more than one thing very well. We're not saying that each of your talents enables you to do *everything* very well, but know that each of them can be applied to multiple areas of achievement.

The great value in your talents is not merely that they help you achieve, but that they help you achieve at levels of *excellence*. Your greatest talents are inextricably linked to your top achievements and to what you do best. Your talents make you exceptional. Therefore, coming to know, understand, and value your talents is directly linked to achieving in classes, careers, and throughout your life.

Talent Versus Other Concepts of Ability

The concept of talent is more specific in terms of the quality it describes and the things that various types of talent help a person to do very well. Traditional concepts and measures of ability (for example, I.Q. and aptitude testing) are more global and are not designed to explain what a person can specifically do.

The concept of talent also goes beyond the limits of traditional concepts of academic abilities (for example, in the areas of reading, math, and composition) in that it also addresses the qualities that help a person achieve in all aspects of life.

The 34 Themes of Talent Measured by the Clifton StrengthsFinder

What is a theme? Essentially, it's is a group of similar talents.

Kerri Strug once again provides a good illustration. Kerri used a wide variety of talents in the Focus theme to achieve in athletics and academics. Among them was her talent for focusing on the precise steps required to perform complicated gymnastic maneuvers, and, during the intense pressure of the Olympics, her talent for blocking out the distraction of intense pain to produce a gold-medal performance.

Kerri used other types of talents, too. Her talents in the Adaptability theme enabled her to achieve excellence in athletics and academics at the same time. Her talent to balance two extremely high priorities, easily moving from one to the other, was crucial to her success in each area.

As a result of studying top achievers for more than three decades, Gallup was able to identify more than 400 themes of talent. The 34 most prevalent themes are measured by StrengthsFinder.

Back to Your Question: What Is a Strength?

Now, let's go to the definition of a strength: A strength is the ability to provide consistent, near-perfect performance in a given activity.

As you read earlier, the concept of strengths begins with talent. Each person naturally has a group of talents. Talents are like "diamonds in the rough," whereas strengths are like diamonds that show brilliance after they have been carefully cut and polished.

Your greatest areas of talent, your most likely sources of potential strengths, are identified by StrengthsFinder.

Just as finished diamonds start as diamonds in the rough, strengths begin with talents. And just as rough diamonds are naturally found in the earth, talents are naturally found within you. But while diamonds are refined with blades and polishing wheels, strengths are produced when talents are refined with *knowledge* and *skill*.

Unlike talent, which must naturally exist within you, skills and knowledge can be acquired. Skills are the basic ability to perform the specific steps of an activity. Knowledge consists of facts and lessons learned.

Many of the skills and much of the knowledge that are combined with talent to create a strength come through experience, and sometimes a great deal of it. Skills and knowledge are also developed in a "book learning" sense, such as in the academic arenas of high school, college, technical school, and training classes.

When you have supplemented your greatest talents with knowledge and skill to the point at which you can provide consistent, near-perfect performance in a given activity, you have a strength. And in applying and even further refining your strengths, you move closer and closer to fulfilling your natural potential as an individual.

Each person has a unique and profound set and combination of talents that are developed and used to different degrees. This combination of talents makes each person like no other.

While each person defines success for himself or herself, achievement and excellence result from fully developing and applying strengths. Some roles require several strengths, all working together, to produce excellence.

You probably already have some strengths, and you certainly will have plenty of opportunity to develop more strengths throughout your lifetime.

What Do Strengths Produce?

As you develop strengths by building on your greatest talents, achievements will naturally follow. But there is also a great sense of personal satisfaction that results from knowing that you are becoming more and more of whom you have the potential to be. In a sense, the development and application of strengths generate a feeling that you are fulfilling your personal destiny. This can produce enormous satisfaction and enhance the quality of your life.

While the experiences of individual people differ tremendously, most report that it is a rewarding experience to be fully living in tune with their natural talents by building and using strengths. Almost everyone says increased confidence and optimism as they become aware of, affirm, and celebrate their talents. Many describe the experience as "coming alive," or even feeling joy as they develop and apply strengths. Reports about the exact inner experiences may differ, but nearly everyone who develops and uses strengths reports a sense of positive and pleasant psychological rewards.

Our initial goal is for you to become more aware of your talents and your potential strengths. We hope you are filled with appreciation for your particular talents, for the positive differences they have already made in your life, and for the excellence strengths can produce in your future achievements, relationships, and other life experiences.

The Beauty of Strengths: Angel's Story

Angel Alcoser is an extraordinarily talented educator. She stands in front of her bilingual kindergarten/first-grade class and performs her role with poise, grace, and excellence — yet with no formal training.

Angel obtained an "emergency credential" to teach the year she graduated from college. She hadn't taken any courses in curriculum design, teaching methods, or assessment. But somehow she knew what to do and performed as if she were a magician generating one creative learning activity after another.

At the beginning of one class, which two visitors were observing, Angel stood before the children and said, "Boys and girls, would you like to perform for our guests?"

With a rousing *"Yes,"* the children lined up.

As Angel walked over to the tape recorder on a table by the wall, every eye was on her. She pushed the "play" button, and with the first note, the children burst into a breathtaking show of song and dance. The visitors were moved, even spellbound.

Angel later explained how she prepared to do her work as an educator. She related a story about the children, the potential she saw in each one of them, and how she tried to involve parents and make her classroom like a family. Then, she talked about how essential it was to connect with every child, emphasizing the importance of seeing each one as a unique person.

"Most of the children in my class come from very humble homes," Angel said. "Some are neglected; some are abused. But," she asserted, "I can't control much of what goes on outside of my class. I do what I can. Once they are in my class, they are all safe. In my class, they can grow to be more than they have ever been."

Angel continued, "I don't focus on what they don't have. I focus on who they are and what they have to offer. I challenge the students to see what they do have, not what they don't. I want them to see that each of them has something that makes them special. They are each talented in some way. Some of the children are great storytellers; others seem to be natural leaders; still others are wonderful organizers. Regardless of the type of talent, I start with the child and what each of them can do best."

How does Angel recognize the children's talents?

"I listen. I look. I see them. I work at it every day! Almost every day, I stay after class. I sit in the classroom and meditate about each child. I let my imagination go and imagine each child both in terms of who they are now and the person they can become."

Angel spoke glowingly about one young lady in her class, who often wore a little blue cap that flopped over her ears. The girl, Delia, carried an old file folder with accordion sides. "She's from a very humble home," Angel said. "It's only her and her mother, who sells oranges on street corners. They are very poor. But Delia has a dream that one day she will become a doctor. Every day, she picks up papers and stuffs them in her little folder. She does this because she pretends that she is already in college and that those papers are the homework assignments for her college classes."

At the end of the school year, Angel presided over the children's graduation ceremony. Each child was encouraged to invite one or more family members, and this really excited the children. More than 30 people attended. The children performed as a group with dance and music, singing alternately in English and Spanish.

The formal graduation ceremony began with the children taking their little chairs and making a large circle in the middle of the room. Angel stepped into the middle of the circle carrying a large box. Then, she called every child's name one by one, and each one went up to the box and pulled out a picture frame containing a piece of paper with printing and handwriting, a picture in the middle, and brightly colored stars around the border.

As the children got their framed pieces of paper, they turned and walked back to their chairs and handed their framed works of art to the parents and other guests they had invited.

At the conclusion of the ceremony, Angel read what was on the framed pieces of paper:

"I was born to dream big dreams. I would like to be _____ when I grow up."

In the blank space, each child wrote his or her goal, the career they hoped to pursue. Then, there was the picture of the child, beneath which these words appeared in bold print: "Yes, I can do it. Give me your unconditional love and tell me every day that I was born to do beautiful things. With much love." And then there was a line where each child wrote his or her name.

The Best of the Best All Have One Thing in Common

Angel Alcoser, in both her excellence in teaching and her approach to students, exemplifies what Gallup has discovered through more than two million in-depth interviews with people from all walks of life: Top achievers in virtually every profession, career, and field of achievement all build their lives upon their talents.

This simple but profound finding forms the heart of this book. You see, Angel isn't one of the "best of the best" by accident. She has achieved excellence because she has capitalized on her talents. In fact, she has built her teaching strategies, even her whole life, on her talents.

Findings From Gallup's Study of the Best

Here is what Gallup knows about top achievers: *They fully recognize their talents and build on them to develop strengths.* In contrast, under-achievers, the merely average, and even above-average achievers often fail to recognize their powerful talents and develop strengths. But the best achievers are certain to do so.

Top achievers apply their greatest talents in roles that best suit them. Clearly, to achieve, one must apply his or her abilities, and many do so to some level of success. But the best apply their most naturally powerful talents and do so in roles that are best suited to those talents. The ability to achieve with excellence in one area is not proof of the ability to perform equally well in another area. A proper "fit" between an individual's talents and the task at hand is essential.

Top achievers invent ways to apply their greatest talents to their achievement tasks. Every role, position, and career entails a group of tasks that must be completed, and quite often the person who performs them must consciously seek, even invent, ways to apply his or her talents to that end — even when one's role is well suited to his or her talents.

How Angel Alcoser Uses Three of Her Signature Themes

Angel took the Clifton StrengthsFinder assessment, which identifies the user's top five themes of talent — their Signature Themes. In both her role as an educator and her personal life, she primarily uses strengths that she has developed from talents in three of her Signature Themes.

1. Maximizer: People exceptionally talented in the Maximizer theme focus on strengths as a way to stimulate personal and group excellence. They seek to transform something strong into something superb.

2. Connectedness: People exceptionally talented in the Connectedness theme have faith in the links between all things. They believe there are few coincidences and that almost every event has a reason.

3. Developer: People exceptionally talented in the Developer theme recognize and cultivate the potential in others. They spot the signs of each small improvement and derive satisfaction from these improvements.

You can easily see how Angel used Maximizer and Developer talents as she worked with the children. Remember that she said that she focused on who the children were, rather than who they weren't. Angel started out with the correct assumption that each child had unique and powerful talents.

Angel's ability to perceive talent in the children, to notice progress, and to mirror what she sees in each child are not coincidences. Angel has an abundance of talent within the Developer and Maximizer themes.

Angel's Connectedness talents are reflected in her determination to connect with children and their families. Connectedness also comes into play as she sets up her classroom with a family atmosphere.

Mostly, Angel's Connectedness talents are revealed in the way she meditates after school and envisions each child. She is looking for talents within each child and for the role she can play in their development. Her Connectedness talents enable her to see a bigger picture, a grand plan.

What makes Angel Alcoser such an outstanding educator starts with who she is as a person. Her natural talents are the source of her excellence. She is simply being her true self. Understand this: Top achievers fully develop whatever talents they happen to possess and apply the resulting strengths in a way that positively impacts their role or the task at hand.

The Tragedy of Undiscovered Talents

Less than five miles from where Angel first taught, there is another elementary school. A young girl by the name of Leonor was a student there in the 1950s. When Leonor was 10 years old, she and her parents emigrated to the United States from Mexico. She had done very well in school in her native country, but she didn't know any English, so classes in the United States would be much more difficult for her. Nevertheless, she was anxious to go to school, because it had always been a positive experience for her in Mexico.

In fact, Leonor had always had a secret desire to become a teacher. She had two great aunts who were teachers, and she greatly admired them. Because she could neither read nor write in English, Leonor was held back and repeated the fourth grade. Her fourth-grade teacher volunteered to stay after school to help her learn English. Leonor worked hard throughout elementary, junior high, and high school. In her sophomore, junior, and senior years, Leonor earned almost straight A's, and each year she was on the honor roll and in the Honors Society. She graduated near the top of her class.

Unfortunately, Leonor never had a teacher like Angel, who could lead her to discover her natural talents. And despite the fact that she was an honor student, no one ever asked if she might be interested in attending college.

The year Leonor graduated from high school, her father lost his job. So Leonor found work in a business close to her home and would turn her paycheck over to her parents so they could pay the rent and buy food for the whole family.

For the next 33 years, Leonor toiled in the banking industry and hated almost every day of it. What's incredibly sad is that Leonor was convinced that she had no talents.

The tragedy for Leonor wasn't in where she worked or what she did. Banking is a fine and respectable profession in which many people thrive and are quite happy; Leonor herself advanced to vice president and administrative manager of a branch office. Clearly, Leonor achieved, and she didn't squander 33 years in banking. But those years could have been immensely more fulfilling if Leonor had been aware of her natural talents. Fortunately, in recent years, Leonor has gone through the process of discovering the talents she has had from the beginning, refining and building on them to create strengths, and applying those strengths. Following her talents, Leonor has transitioned from banking into teaching, where she is experiencing joy and excitement like she never has before.

Your Strengths Quest Begins With You

As described earlier, the seeds of your personal greatness — your talents — are already in you. Therefore, your strengths quest — your quest to achieve excellence and become all you can be through your own natural talents — is really a quest to discover, develop, and apply who you truly are. Your strengths quest begins as you look within yourself as an individual to recognize your own natural talents.

Your quest will then continue as you build on your talents to develop strengths — abilities to provide consistent, near-perfect performances in specific activities. As you do this, your self-identity and personal values should become clearer, and as a result, you will likely become more confident, optimistic, and focused. As you achieve through your greatest talents, you will likely aspire to higher goals.

Your strengths quest is a lifelong adventure. Each of the three aspects — discovery, development, and application — will continue throughout your life. This exciting and fulfilling process should bring you a lifetime of great satisfaction and joy.

Chapter II

GAINING DIRECTION
FOR YOUR QUEST

A strengths quest is a revolutionary approach to achieving. Why? Because adopting a strengths perspective to your life and fully embracing it has a radical impact on your motivation. So, what exactly are the connections between your strengths quest and your motivations?

1. **Your quest addresses your questions.**

   Most great scholars know that motivation to conduct research, and to learn in general, stems from personally meaningful questions to which they want to find answers.

2. **Your quest is an adventure of discovery.**

   A quest is motivating simply because of the adventure and the discoveries you will make along the way. The first adventure is discovering your talents — but that is only the beginning. Then, there are discoveries and insights that will come to you as you gain a strengths perspective on your entire life. Suddenly, you will begin to understand the connection between your talents and your past achievements.

3. **Your quest generates optimism.**

   As you become increasingly aware of your talents, you'll develop more optimistic, because you realize that you have abilities you can use in pursuing your goals. This alone builds motivation because you recognize that in your talents, you in fact have assets that can help you reach your desired goals.

4. **Your quest provides a sense of direction.**

   Being lost is a dreadful experience. One of the most motivating aspects of a strengths quest is the increased sense of direction that comes as you gain a greater understanding of who you are.

5. **Your quest generates confidence.**

   As you become increasingly aware of your talents and as you develop strengths, you will become more aware of your potential for excellence. As a result, you'll gain confidence.

6. **Your quest generates a sense of vitality.**

Whenever you use your greatest talents, there is a psychological reward — you receive both satisfaction and motivation. The pleasurable experience of using those talents seems to reach some of your deepest motivations. When you are using your most natural talents, you seem to become more fully alive.

Your Signature Themes Report

Let's turn now to your Signature Themes report, which you received after completing the Clifton StrengthsFinder assessment.

As described earlier, your Signature Themes are your five most dominant themes of talent, as indicated by your responses to the assessment. They are presented in rank order, with your most dominant theme listed first. Each Signature Theme is accompanied by a description of the talents in that theme.

Some people are concerned about receiving only their top five themes. That's understandable, but Gallup research clearly points to the fact that the top achievers focus on their most dominant areas of talent, and we would like you to do the same. Attempting to focus on too many themes can dilute the attention you give to your top themes. Also, we don't want you to fall prey to the conventional "wisdom" that the best way to achieve is to emphasize your areas of lesser talent. We want you to hone in on your Signature Themes — your greatest areas of talent — which present your best opportunities to achieve.

What Should You Do With Your Signature Themes Report?

The rest of this book is devoted to answering this question. But there are two things that we would like you to do as soon as possible.

First, please print a copy of your report, and carefully read the descriptions of each of your Signature Themes. Please underline or highlight each term, phrase, and sentence that seems to describe you.

Next, contact the three people who know you best, and read each of your Signature Themes and their descriptions. After reading each description, please ask these people if they see that theme in you. If they say yes, ask them to give you an example of when they have seen it in you. If any of them answer no, simply move on to the next Signature Theme.

You are a talented person with a unique and very special set of talents. Now, it's time to learn more about them and gain further direction for your strengths quest by affirming your Signature Themes.

Chapter III

AFFIRMING AND CELEBRATING
YOUR TALENTS

You have taken the Clifton StrengthsFinder, received your Signature Themes report, and discussed your Signature Themes with three people who know you very well. Now, it's time for you to affirm the Signature Themes indicated by your StrengthsFinder responses.

Affirming a Signature Theme simply means that you *agree* that it is one of your dominant areas of talent. It also means being able to see how your talent in that theme enables you to do certain things very well. Affirming your Signature Themes may seem easy, but many people experience some difficulty in doing so. Listed below are some of those difficulties and the reasons for them.

Difficulties in Affirming Our Signature Themes

1. *Many people are blind to their own greatest talents, and often to the greatest talents of others.* Some of our talents are called upon so frequently that we take them for granted. We don't consider them special, and we don't even perceive them as talents. Consequently, our Signature Themes may not seem important, valuable, or even special to us.

2. *Our talents sometimes threaten others. Rather than admit their insecurity, some people criticize us for having talents they wish they had.* As a result, we might mistakenly come to think that our Signature Themes hold weaknesses rather than talents.

3. *In some cases, we end up in positions or roles that simply don't fit our dominant talents.* Or, those talents may conflict with the roles and expectations of the positions we are in. This can make us feel like there is something wrong with us. But the problem may only be a mismatch between our dominant talents and the expectations of a role we are in.

4. *The fear of becoming proud and arrogant may interfere with seeing and affirming our Signature Themes.* In reality, pride and arrogance often stem from feelings of inadequacy. Affirming our dominant areas of talent usually results in humble gratitude for having been blessed with them.

5. *Some people have difficulty affirming their Signature Themes because they don't see how the talents in them will help them achieve*

their goals. If that is the case, they will benefit from a better understanding of their talents. Talents are always valuable, and they can often be applied toward achievement in less obvious, or even surprising, ways.

Questions You Might Be Asking

If a Particular Theme Is Not Among Your Signature Themes, Is It Necessarily an Area of Weakness?

No. The Clifton StrengthsFinder *does not* simultaneously measure weakness and talent. StrengthsFinder measures talent, and that's all it does. So, if a particular theme is not among your Signature Themes, it simply means that at least five other themes are more dominant in you. For example, your Responsibility theme might not be among your Signature Themes. That doesn't mean you are irresponsible. It just means that your overall talents in at least five other themes are more dominant than those in your Responsibility theme.

By focusing on your Signature Themes, you will concentrate your attention on where you have the greatest potential for achieving excellence and personal fulfillment. Focusing on any other area may serve as nothing more than a distraction.

What If You Believe You Have Dominant Talent in a Theme That Was Not Identified as a Signature Theme?

Our response is simple and direct: Claim it! Affirm and celebrate your talents in that theme, then build on them to fully develop and apply strengths. Just remember that we limited your Signature Themes to five because focusing on your *most* dominant areas of talent will provide the greatest opportunities for achievement.

Is Having Talent Always a Positive Experience?

Talent is always positive in the sense that it enables a person to do certain things very well. Your talents always hold potential for positive results in terms of achievements, success, personal fulfillment, and a better quality of life.

At the same time, talents place demands on the people who have them. And from that standpoint, talents can present a bit of a challenge.

Some people honestly say that they wish that their talents weren't so powerful in certain themes because they make their lives more demanding. They simply may experience more pressure because other people place higher expectations on them to achieve.

AFFIRMING YOUR
SIGNATURE THEMES

Affirming Your Signature Themes While Acknowledging Challenges They May Pose

On your Signature Themes report, each of your Signature Themes is accompanied by a paragraph that describes talents often found within that theme. While some of the talents described may not fit you, many of them should sound very familiar — and that is what is important. The issue is not who you *aren't*; the issue is who you *are* in terms of your dominant talents.

At this point, we would like you to consider insights and action ideas for affirming your Signature Themes. Items for each of the 34 themes measured by the Clifton StrengthsFinder are presented here, in alphabetical order by theme. Please locate and examine the items that are customized to your Signature Themes.

The first few items listed under each theme describe some of the key talents in the theme, and might touch on a challenge that talents from that theme can present, such as how they may be misjudged or misperceived by others. The final item touches on the "genius" of the theme that makes its talents so valuable. By "genius" we mean an extraordinary ability.

Achiever as One of Your Signature Themes

To begin affirming Achiever as one of your areas of dominant talents, first take another look at the description of that theme:

Your Achiever theme helps explain your drive. Achiever describes a constant need for achievement. You feel as if every day starts at zero. By the end of the day you must achieve something tangible in order to feel good about yourself. And by "every day" you mean every single day — workdays, weekends, vacations. No matter how much you may feel you deserve a day of rest, if the day passes without some form of achievement, no matter how small, you will feel dissatisfied. You have an internal fire burning inside you. It pushes you to do more, to achieve more. After each accomplishment is reached, the fire dwindles for a moment, but very soon it rekindles itself, forcing you toward the next accomplishment. Your relentless need for achievement might not be logical. It might not even be focused. But it will always be with you. As an Achiever you must learn to live with this whisper of discontent. It does have its benefits. It brings you the energy you need to work long hours without burning out. It is the jolt you can always count on to get you started on new tasks, new challenges. It is the power supply that causes you to set the pace and define the levels of productivity for your work group. It is the theme that keeps you moving.

Now, consider this statement based on comments from individuals who possess Achiever among their Signature Themes. It represents what Achiever could "sound like."

"Instead of just fifteen credit hours each semester, I'm going to take eighteen or twenty so I can graduate even sooner and get started in my career."

For further understanding of your talents, examine these insights and select those that describe you best.

☐ You work very hard to complete each task on your "to do" list, and you always have a long list. In fact, at the end of the day some achievers add to their list all of the unexpected tasks they've accomplished, just so they have the satisfaction of crossing them off the list.

☐ You are busy and productive, and you derive satisfaction from your accomplishments.

☐ You can draw on a deep reservoir of internal motivation, stamina, and determination to achieve your goals.

☐ Other people may criticize you, because to them you seem too driven to achieve. They may call you a "workaholic" but the truth is that you like your work, and you like to work hard.

The genius of Achiever talents is your sheer ability to push hard to get things done. You are known for that.

Activator as One of Your Signature Themes

To begin affirming Activator as one of your areas of dominant talents, first take another look at the description of that theme:

"When can we start?" This is a recurring question in your life. You are impatient for action. You may concede that analysis has its uses or that debate and discussion can occasionally yield some valuable insights, but deep down you know that only action is real. Only action can make things happen. Only action leads to performance. Once a decision is made, you cannot not act. Others may worry that "there are still some things we don't know," but this doesn't seem to slow you. If the decision has been made to go across town, you know that the fastest way to get there is to go stoplight to stoplight. You are not going to sit around waiting until all the lights have turned green. Besides, in your view, action and thinking are not opposites. In fact, guided by your Activator theme, you believe that action is the best device for learning. You make a decision, you take action, you look at the result, and you learn. This learning informs your next action and your next. How can you grow if you have nothing to react to? Well, you believe you can't. You must put yourself out there. You must take the next step. It is the only way to keep your thinking fresh and informed. The bottom line is this: You know you will be judged not by what you say, not by what you think, but by what you get done. This does not frighten you. It pleases you.

Now, consider this statement based on comments from individuals who possess Activator among their Signature Themes. It represents what Activator could "sound like."

"On our group project for Sociology class, things just weren't getting done — nothing was moving. I decided to get everyone together to get the ball rolling again."

For further understanding of your talents, examine these insights and select those that describe you best.

☐ You naturally see how ideas can be turned into action.

☐ You want to do things now, rather than simply talk about them.

☐ You can be very powerful in making things happen and getting people to take action.

☐ Other people may criticize you for being impatient and seeming to "run over" them. You might occasionally struggle with people you feel are trying to control you.

The genius of Activator talents is in your natural ability to initiate the transformation of ideas into actions, programs, and services.

Adaptability as One of Your Signature Themes

To begin affirming Adaptability as one of your areas of dominant talents, first take another look at the description of that theme:

You live in the moment. You don't see the future as a fixed destination. Instead, you see it as a place that you create out of the choices that you make right now. And so you discover your future one choice at a time. This doesn't mean that you don't have plans. You probably do. But this theme of Adaptability does enable you to respond willingly to the demands of the moment even if they pull you away from your plans. Unlike some, you don't resent sudden requests or unforeseen detours. You expect them. They are inevitable. Indeed, on some level you actually look forward to them. You are, at heart, a very flexible person who can stay productive when the demands of work are pulling you in many different directions at once.

Now, consider this statement based on comments from individuals who possess Adaptability among their Signature Themes. It represents what Adaptability could "sound like."

"My friends know that I am willing and able to drop everything in order to help them. I can change my schedule at a moment's notice, so when people need something from me, it doesn't stress me out."

For further understanding of your talents, examine these insights and select those that describe you best.

☐ In many ways, you modify yourself to meet the demands of your environment.

☐ You easily adjust to many things all day long because you naturally live in the moment.

☐ You create the future out of the choices you make right now, one choice at a time.

☐ Your "go with the flow" attitude may seem like irresponsibility to those who prefer structure and predictability. They may get irritated with what they perceive to be sloppiness or carelessness.

☐ Adaptability talents are valuable because they allow you to keep moving forward when the unexpected happens. You can press ahead in a world of unknowns and seemingly unfair treatment when others would give up. You can deal with everything from injustices to crises and still find a way to make progress.

The genius of Adaptability talents lies in the way you respond to chaos: You can quickly change and respond in circumstances that would be frightening or intimidating to others.

Analytical as One of Your Signature Themes

To begin affirming Analytical as one of your areas of dominant talents, first take another look at the description of that theme:

Your Analytical theme challenges other people: "Prove it. Show me why what you are claiming is true." In the face of this kind of questioning some will find that their brilliant theories wither and die. For you, this is precisely the point. You do not necessarily want to destroy other people's ideas, but you do insist that their theories be sound. You see yourself as objective and dispassionate. You like data because they are value free. They have no agenda. Armed with these data, you search for patterns and connections. You want to understand how certain patterns affect one another. How do they combine? What is their outcome? Does this outcome fit with the theory being offered or the situation being confronted? These are your questions. You peel the layers back until, gradually, the root cause or causes are revealed. Others see you as logical and rigorous. Over time they will come to you in order to expose someone's "wishful thinking" or "clumsy thinking" to your refining mind. It is hoped that your analysis is never delivered too harshly. Otherwise, others may avoid you when that "wishful thinking" is their own.

Now, consider this statement based on comments from individuals who possess Analytical among their Signature Themes. It represents what Analytical could "sound like."

"One of the things I love about my philosophy class is that the professor encourages us to challenge what we are learning. I love to pick apart an argument, ask questions, and debate the evidence."

For further understanding of your talents, examine these insights and select those that describe you best.

☐ You search for the reasons why things are the way they are.

☐ You think about the factors that might affect a situation and what causes certain reactions.

☐ You take a more critical approach to what others might quickly accept as truth. You want to see the proof.

☐ Some people may reject you and your questioning ways because you insist that facts be verified, theories be sound, and reasoning be logical. Some people may feel you are negative or unnecessarily critical when, from your standpoint, you are simply trying to understand something.

☐ Analytical talents are valuable because they enable you to dig deep, find the root causes and effects, and then develop clear thoughts based on facts. This type of thinking helps you gain clarity about excellence and how it can be attained.

The genius of Analytical talents lies in the solid foundation you lay for moving forward. Your questions drive you to uncover the essential facts needed for excellence in any endeavor.

Arranger as One of Your Signature Themes

To begin affirming Arranger as one of your areas of dominant talents, first take another look at the description of that theme:

You are a conductor. When faced with a complex situation involving many factors, you enjoy managing all of the variables, aligning and realigning them until you are sure you have arranged them in the most productive configuration possible. In your mind there is nothing special about what you are doing. You are simply trying to figure out the best way to get things done. But others, lacking this theme, will be in awe of your ability. "How can you keep so many things in your head at once?" they will ask. "How can you stay so flexible, so willing to shelve well-laid plans in favor of some brand-new configuration that has just occurred to you?" But you cannot imagine behaving in any other way. You are a shining example of effective flexibility, whether you are changing travel schedules at the last minute because a better fare has popped up or mulling over just the right combination of people and resources to accomplish a new project. From the mundane to the complex, you are always looking for the perfect configuration. Of course, you are at your best in dynamic situations. Confronted with the unexpected, some complain that plans devised with such care cannot be changed, while others take refuge in the existing rules or procedures. You don't do either. Instead, you jump into the confusion, devising new options, hunting for new paths of least resistance, and figuring out new partnerships — because, after all, there might just be a better way.

Now, consider this statement based on comments from individuals who possess Arranger among their Signature Themes. It represents what Arranger could "sound like."

"The school year is wrapping up, which means that I have to study for finals and prepare to move out of the dorms, in addition to working my part-time job. Not a problem. I'll ask my boss to schedule me to work the days before my easier exams, which will give me more time to study for the tough ones. I'll pack during my study breaks."

For further understanding of your talents, examine these insights and select those that describe you best.

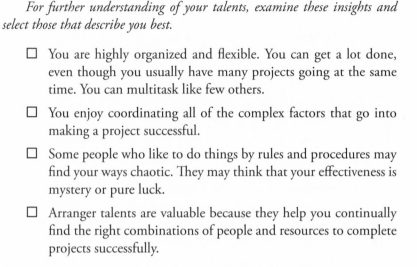

☐ You are highly organized and flexible. You can get a lot done, even though you usually have many projects going at the same time. You can multitask like few others.

☐ You enjoy coordinating all of the complex factors that go into making a project successful.

☐ Some people who like to do things by rules and procedures may find your ways chaotic. They may think that your effectiveness is mystery or pure luck.

☐ Arranger talents are valuable because they help you continually find the right combinations of people and resources to complete projects successfully.

The genius of Arranger talents lies in your ability to orchestrate people and resources for maximum effectiveness.

Belief as One of Your Signature Themes

To begin affirming Belief as one of your areas of dominant talents, first take another look at the description of that theme:

If you possess a strong Belief theme, you have certain core values that are enduring. These values vary from one person to another, but ordinarily your Belief theme causes you to be family-oriented, altruistic, even spiritual, and to value responsibility and high ethics — both in yourself and others. These core values affect your behavior in many ways. They give your life meaning and satisfaction; in your view, success is more than money and prestige. They provide you with direction, guiding you through the temptations and distractions of life toward a consistent set of priorities. This consistency is the foundation for all your relationships. Your friends call you dependable. "I know where you stand," they say. Your Belief makes you easy to trust. It also demands that you find work that meshes with your values. Your work must be meaningful; it must matter to you. And guided by your Belief theme it will matter only if it gives you a chance to live out your values.

Now, consider this statement based on comments from individuals who possess Belief among their Signature Themes. It represents what Belief could "sound like."

"My education is important to me, but making a difference for the kids in my community is part of my personal mission. Even when I have a lot of assignments due, I make time to volunteer for the after-school program at the youth center."

For further understanding of your talents, examine these insights and select those that describe you best.

☐ You have core values that are unchanging. You may conflict with people who oppose or don't value your beliefs.

☐ You have deeply held ideas about what is, what should be, and the purpose of your life.

☐ You naturally become enthusiastic and energetic about tasks, roles, or positions that promote your deeply held beliefs.

☐ Some people may think you are rigid or contrary because of your strongly held beliefs.

☐ When you live your life according to your deepest values and beliefs, you experience motivation, drive, and determination.

The genius of Belief talents is found in the tremendous power of your foundational values. They are sources of powerful drive and direction.

Command as One of Your Signature Themes

To begin affirming Command as one of your areas of dominant talents, first take another look at the description of that theme:

Command leads you to take charge. Unlike some people, you feel no discomfort with imposing your views on others. On the contrary, once your opinion is formed, you need to share it with others. Once your goal is set, you feel restless until you have aligned others with you. You are not frightened by confrontation; rather, you know that confrontation is the first step toward resolution. Whereas others may avoid facing up to life's unpleasantness, you feel compelled to present the facts or the truth, no matter how unpleasant it may be. You need things to be clear between people and challenge them to be clear-eyed and honest. You push them to take risks. You may even intimidate them. And while some may resent this, labeling you opinionated, they often willingly hand you the reins. People are drawn toward those who take a stance and ask them to move in a certain direction. Therefore, people will be drawn to you. You have presence. You have Command.

Now, consider this statement based on comments from individuals who possess Command among their Signature Themes. It represents what Command could "sound like."

"Some of my friends are intimidated by conflict, but not me. If I'm upset with someone or see something that isn't right, I'll say so! People know what I think. I'm not a hard person to read."

For further understanding of your talents, examine these insights and select those that describe you best.

- ☐ You see what needs to be done, and you are willing to say so.

- ☐ You are willing to go into a confrontation and argue because you know that what is right will prevail, and confrontations often help get things moving.

- ☐ You can jump into a conflict, crisis, or emergency and take charge of the situation.

- ☐ Other people may feel threatened or put off by your power and assertiveness. When others label you as bossy, it points out an opportunity to manage and develop your Command talents.

- ☐ Command talents are valuable because they help you positively impact other people. You can help people and entire organizations get through difficult times and make substantive changes in the midst of chaos.

The genius of Command talents is in your ability to bring to light what is often avoided or unstated, so that people are able to resolve conflicts and misunderstandings.

Communication as One of Your Signature Themes

To begin affirming Communication as one of your areas of dominant talents, first take another look at the description of that theme:

You like to explain, to describe, to host, to speak in public, and to write. This is your Communication theme at work. Ideas are a dry beginning. Events are static. You feel a need to bring them to life, to energize them, to make them exciting and vivid. And so you turn events into stories and practice telling them. You take the dry idea and enliven it with images and examples and metaphors. You believe that most people have a very short attention span. They are bombarded by information, but very little of it survives. You want your information — whether an idea, an event, a product's features and benefits, a discovery, or a lesson — to survive. You want to divert their attention toward you and then capture it, lock it in. This is what drives your hunt for the perfect phrase. This is what draws you toward dramatic words and powerful word combinations. This is why people like to listen to you. Your word pictures pique their interest, sharpen their world, and inspire them to act.

Now, consider this statement based on comments from individuals who possess Communication among their Signature Themes. It represents what Communication could "sound like."

"When I was a kid, I used to get in trouble for talking in class. But I could tell such great stories — and when my classmates would laugh, it encouraged me to keep talking. My teachers said I was 'a joy to work with,' but that I was disrupting the class."

For further understanding of your talents, examine these insights and select those that describe you best.

- ☐ You like to talk, and you probably are good at it.
- ☐ You can explain things and make them clear.
- ☐ You may have an ability to tell particularly captivating stories by constructing mental images in the minds of others.
- ☐ You may be criticized because you like to talk a lot.

☐ Communication talents are valuable because your abilities in this area enable you to reach out and connect with people. Your storytelling ability builds images in the minds of others and makes you a powerful person as you connect and bond with people.

The genius of Communication talents lies in your ability to find words for not only your own thoughts and feelings, but also those of others.

Competition as One of Your Signature Themes

To begin affirming Competition as one of your areas of dominant talents, first take another look at the description of that theme:

Competition is rooted in comparison. When you look at the world, you are instinctively aware of other people's performance. Their performance is the ultimate yardstick. No matter how hard you tried, no matter how worthy your intentions, if you reached your goal but did not outperform your peers, the achievement feels hollow. Like all competitors, you need other people. You need to compare. If you can compare, you can compete, and if you can compete, you can win. And when you win, there is no feeling quite like it. You like measurement because it facilitates comparisons. You like other competitors because they invigorate you. You like contests because they must produce a winner. You particularly like contests where you know you have the inside track to be the winner. Although you are gracious to your fellow competitors and even stoic in defeat, you don't compete for the fun of competing. You compete to win. Over time you will come to avoid contests where winning seems unlikely.

Now, consider this statement based on comments from individuals who possess Competition among their Signature Themes. It represents what Competition could "sound like."

"I like to know where I stand in a class. I like it when the professor posts the grades and I can see that I'm at the top. Competing against my classmates motivates me — and when I can't do that, I even compete against myself and try to do better than I did last time."

For further understanding of your talents, examine these insights and select those that describe you best.

☐ You want to win, which usually means outperforming others.

☐ You will work hard to excel — especially in comparison to others.

☐ You constantly compare yourself and your performance to other people and their performances.

☐ You may not be willing to try something if you think you can't "win" at it. Other people may consider your competitiveness inappropriate and therefore push you away, reject you, or accuse you of being arrogant.

The genius of Competition talents lies in your ability to stimulate yourself and others to higher levels of performance.

Connectedness as One of Your Signature Themes

To begin affirming Connectedness as one of your areas of dominant talents, first take another look at the description of that theme:

Things happen for a reason. You are sure of it. You are sure of it because in your soul you know that we are all connected. Yes, we are individuals, responsible for our own judgments and in possession of our own free will, but nonetheless we are part of something larger. Some may call it the collective unconscious. Others may label it spirit or life force. But whatever your word of choice, you gain confidence from knowing that we are not isolated from one another or from the earth and the life on it. This feeling of Connectedness implies certain responsibilities. If we are all part of a larger picture, then we must not harm others because we will be harming ourselves. We must not exploit because we will be exploiting ourselves. Your awareness of these responsibilities creates your value system. You are considerate, caring, and accepting. Certain of the unity of humankind, you are a bridge builder for people of different cultures. Sensitive to the invisible hand, you can give others comfort that there is a purpose beyond our humdrum lives. The exact articles of your faith will depend on your upbringing and your culture, but your faith is strong. It sustains you and your close friends in the face of life's mysteries.

Now, consider this statement based on comments from individuals who possess Connectedness among their Signature Themes. It represents what Connectedness could "sound like."

"There's a reason I'm so committed to caring for the environment. We're all part of the earth, so if I don't do my part to take care of it, we all suffer."

For further understanding of your talents, examine these insights and select those that describe you best.

☐ You see that all things happen for a reason. You believe that all things are working together in a purposeful manner.

☐ You feel connected to life itself. Therefore, you feel a responsibility to be considerate, caring, and accepting toward others.

☐ You build bridges that allow people from all backgrounds to come together and develop a faith that goes beyond themselves.

☐ When people and the world seem fractured, broken, and isolated, you can become discouraged. For this reason, some may perceive you as too naïve or fragile.

☐ Connectedness talents are valuable because they provide you with conviction and faith that sustain and encourage you and your friends in difficult times. You believe that there's a plan, a design, and a power beyond the visible world that provide meaning, comfort, and confidence.

The genius of Connectedness talents lies in the ability to "connect the dots" between the past, present, and future in a way that gives you and others hope.

Consistency as One of Your Signature Themes

To begin affirming Consistency as one of your areas of dominant talents, first take another look at the description of that theme:

Balance is important to you. You are keenly aware of the need to treat people the same, no matter what their station in life, so you do not want to see the scales tipped too far in any one person's favor. In your view this leads to selfishness and individualism. It leads to a world where some people gain an unfair advantage because of their connections or their background or their greasing of the wheels. This is truly offensive to you. You see yourself as a guardian against it. In direct contrast to this world of special favors, you believe that people function best in a consistent environment where the rules are clear and are applied to everyone equally. This is an environment where people know what is expected. It is predictable and evenhanded. It is fair. Here each person has an even chance to show his or her worth.

Now, consider this statement based on comments from individuals who possess Consistency among their Signature Themes. It represents what Consistency could "sound like."

"In one of my classes, we were each assigned a different book to read. But some of the books had three hundred pages, while others had only one hundred. I wasn't very happy about that because I thought everyone should have to read the same book, or at least the same number of pages."

For further understanding of your talents, examine these insights and select those that describe you best.

☐ You try to treat everyone equally by having clear rules and applying them consistently.

☐ You're offended when some people gain an advantage because of their connections or the "games" they play.

☐ You believe that people work best in a consistent environment where the rules apply to everyone equally, and you work to create that type of environment.

☐ While you may see yourself as a guardian of what is right and a warrior against special treatment, some people may reject you for assuming that responsibility.

The genius of Consistency talents lies in the way you easily and quickly make judgments that equally apply to everyone involved. As a result, people have confidence in you and see you as trustworthy.

Context as One of Your Signature Themes

To begin affirming Context as one of your areas of dominant talents, first take another look at the description of that theme:

You look back. You look back because that is where the answers lie. You look back to understand the present. From your vantage point the present is unstable, a confusing clamor of competing voices. It is only by casting your mind back to an earlier time, a time when the plans were being drawn up, that the present regains its stability. The earlier time was a simpler time. It was a time of blueprints. As you look back, you begin to see these blueprints emerge. You realize what the initial intentions were. These blueprints or intentions have since become so embellished that they are almost unrecognizable, but now this Context theme reveals them again. This understanding brings you confidence. No longer disoriented, you make better decisions because you sense the underlying structure. You become a better partner because you understand how your colleagues came to be who they are. And counterintuitively you become wiser about the future because you saw its seeds being sown in the past. Faced with new people and new situations, it will take you a little time to orient yourself, but you must give yourself this time. You must discipline yourself to ask the questions and allow the blueprints to emerge because no matter what the situation, if you haven't seen the blueprints, you will have less confidence in your decisions.

Now, consider this statement based on comments from individuals who possess Context among their Signature Themes. It represents what Context could "sound like."

"I always think about that saying, 'Those who cannot remember the past are condemned to repeat it.' That's very true, but it's also important to remember the successes of the past so we can learn from them as well."

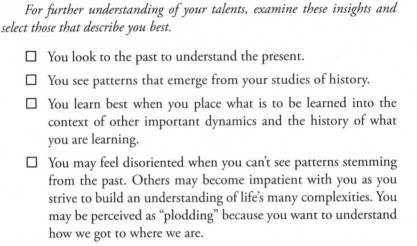

For further understanding of your talents, examine these insights and select those that describe you best.

☐ You look to the past to understand the present.

☐ You see patterns that emerge from your studies of history.

☐ You learn best when you place what is to be learned into the context of other important dynamics and the history of what you are learning.

☐ You may feel disoriented when you can't see patterns stemming from the past. Others may become impatient with you as you strive to build an understanding of life's many complexities. You may be perceived as "plodding" because you want to understand how we got to where we are.

The genius of Context talents is reflected in your unique ability to remember the past and to appreciate that the seeds of "new" are often found in the old.

Deliberative as One of Your Signature Themes

To begin affirming Deliberative as one of your areas of dominant talents, first take another look at the description of that theme:

You are careful. You are vigilant. You are a private person. You know that the world is an unpredictable place. Everything may seem in order, but beneath the surface you sense the many risks. Rather than denying these risks, you draw each one out into the open. Then each risk can be identified, assessed, and ultimately reduced. Thus, you are a fairly serious person who approaches life with a certain reserve. For example, you like to plan ahead so as to anticipate what might go wrong. You select your friends cautiously and keep your own counsel when the conversation turns to personal matters. You are careful not to give too much praise and recognition, lest it be misconstrued. If some people don't like you because you are not as effusive as others, then so be it. For you, life is not a popularity contest. Life is something of a minefield. Others can run through it recklessly if they so choose, but you take a different approach. You identify the dangers, weigh their relative impact, and then place your feet deliberately. You walk with care.

Now, consider this statement based on comments from individuals who possess Deliberative among their Signature Themes. It represents what Deliberative could "sound like."

"My friends couldn't believe the process I went through to choose a college to attend. I took two years to explore all the possibilities and consider any potential barriers — but I needed to be absolutely sure that I wouldn't have any regrets."

For further understanding of your talents, examine these five insights and select those that describe you best.

☐ You take great care as you consider options, thinking through the pros and cons of each alternative. To you, making the correct choice is more important than the time it takes to do so.

☐ You prefer to listen to others rather than reveal a lot of information about yourself. Listening is an important way for you to gather the information you need to make a sound decision.

☐ You make very good decisions. In fact, you would change few of them.

☐ Others may become impatient with you as you make your decisions thoughtfully and slowly. You always think about the risks and what might go wrong. You may be falsely categorized as indecisive when in fact you are making better choices in the long run.

The genius of Deliberative talents is in your ability to reduce risk and prevent problems through innate anticipation and careful thought. As a result, you tend to make outstanding decisions.

Developer as One of Your Signature Themes

To begin affirming Developer as one of your areas of dominant talents, first take another look at the description of that theme:

You see the potential in others. Very often, in fact, potential is all you see. In your view no individual is fully formed. On the contrary, each individual is a work in progress, alive with possibilities. And you are drawn toward people for this very reason. When you interact with others, your goal is to help them experience success. You look for ways to challenge them. You devise interesting experiences that can stretch them and help them grow. And all the while you are on the lookout for the signs of growth — a new behavior learned or modified, a slight improvement in a skill, a glimpse of excellence or of "flow" where previously there were only halting steps. For you these small increments — invisible to some — are clear signs of potential being realized. These signs of growth in others are your fuel. They bring you strength and satisfaction. Over time many will seek you out for help and encouragement because on some level they know that your helpfulness is both genuine and fulfilling to you.

Now, consider this statement based on comments from individuals who possess Developer among their Signature Themes. It represents what Developer could "sound like."

"I am so excited about becoming a teacher. I look at children and see how much of a future they have, and I just love those moments when I see a child make even just a little bit of progress. That's my reward."

For further understanding of your talents, examine these insights and select those that describe you best.

- ☐ You naturally see others' potential to move, change, grow, and develop for the better.
- ☐ You love to see others make progress, and you will notice even the slightest progress.

☐ Being a part of another person's development is the one of best experiences in the world for you.

☐ Other people may not be as interested in their development as you are. In fact, they might push you away because they feel you are pressuring them.

The genius of Developer talents lie in your ability to see the raw potential and incremental progress of others, and to actively invest in furthering that development.

Discipline as One of Your Signature Themes

To begin affirming Discipline as one of your areas of dominant talents, first take another look at the description of that theme:

Your world needs to be predictable. It needs to be ordered and planned. So you instinctively impose structure on your world. You set up routines. You focus on timelines and deadlines. You break long-term projects into a series of specific short-term plans, and you work through each plan diligently. You are not necessarily neat and clean, but you do need precision. Faced with the inherent messiness of life, you want to feel in control. The routines, the timelines, the structure, all of these help create this feeling of control. Lacking this theme of Discipline, others may sometimes resent your need for order, but there need not be conflict. You must understand that not everyone feels your urge for predictability; they have other ways of getting things done. Likewise, you can help them understand and even appreciate your need for structure. Your dislike of surprises, your impatience with errors, your routines, and your detail orientation don't need to be misinterpreted as controlling behaviors that box people in. Rather, these behaviors can be understood as your instinctive method for maintaining your progress and your productivity in the face of life's many distractions.

Now, consider this statement based on comments from individuals who possess Discipline among their Signature Themes. It represents what Discipline could "sound like."

"I'm super-organized. Everything has a place so I know where to find it. My schedule is mapped out in advance, and that enables me to get a lot done. I never miss turning in an assignment on time."

For further understanding of your talents, examine these insights and select those that describe you best.

☐ You find ways to organize yourself to get things done on time.

☐ You tend to place yourself in productive environments.

☐ You create order and structure where it is needed.

☐ Some people may label you as compulsive, anal, or a control freak because of your ability to discipline yourself and structure your world. But these attributes make you productive — often more so than your critics.

The genius of Discipline talents is in your ordered and structured approach, which brings predictability to your work and life.

Empathy as One of Your Signature Themes

To begin affirming Empathy as one of your areas of dominant talents, first take another look at the description of that theme:

You can sense the emotions of those around you. You can feel what they are feeling as though their feelings are your own. Intuitively, you are able to see the world through their eyes and share their perspective. You do not necessarily agree with each person's perspective. You do not necessarily feel pity for each person's predicament — this would be sympathy, not Empathy. You do not necessarily condone the choices each person makes, but you do understand. This instinctive ability to understand is powerful. You hear the unvoiced questions. You anticipate the need. Where others grapple for words, you seem to find the right words and the right tone. You help people find the right phrases to express their feelings — to themselves as well as to others. You help them give voice to their emotional life. For all these reasons other people are drawn to you.

Now, consider this statement based on comments from individuals who possess Empathy among their Signature Themes. It represents what Empathy could "sound like."

"I'm the one my friends turn to when they have a fight with their boyfriend or girlfriend. They know I understand how they're feeling, but they know I can help them see how the other person is feeling, too. I tend to be the one whose shoulder they cry on."

For further understanding of your talents, examine these insights and select those that describe you best.

☐ You can sense what it feels like to be someone else.

☐ You can pick up on the pain and joy of others — sometimes before they express it. Other people feel heard by you and experience your compassion.

☐ Because you can quickly understand others, people are drawn to you when they have a need or a problem, especially in relationships.

☐ Your Empathy can be challenging because you may become overwhelmed with all of the emotions you can pick up in a day.

The genius of Empathy talents lies in the emotional depth of the relationships you're able to form with others. People feel understood by you and seek your company.

Focus as One of Your Signature Themes

To begin affirming Focus as one of your areas of dominant talents, first take another look at the description of that theme:

"Where am I headed?" you ask yourself. You ask this question every day. Guided by this theme of Focus, you need a clear destination. Lacking one, your life and your work can quickly become frustrating. And so each year, each month, and even each week you set goals. These goals then serve as your compass, helping you determine priorities and make the necessary corrections to get back on course. Your Focus is powerful because it forces you to filter; you instinctively evaluate whether or not a particular action will help you move toward your goal. Those that don't are ignored. In the end, then, your Focus forces you to be efficient. Natu-rally, the flip side of this is that it causes you to become impatient with delays, obstacles, and even tangents, no matter how intriguing they appear to be. This makes you an extremely valuable team member. When others start to wander down other avenues, you bring them back to the main road. Your Focus reminds everyone that if something is not help-ing you move toward your destination, then it is not important. And if it is not important, then it is not worth your time. You keep everyone on point.

Now, consider this statement based on comments from individuals who possess Focus among their Signature Themes. It represents what Focus could "sound like."

"Sometimes I'm so intent on my homework that my roommate can walk into the room and say my name — and I don't even realize he's there. I get so zoned in on what I'm doing that nothing breaks my concentration."

For further understanding of your talents, examine these insights and select those that describe you best.

- ☐ You can take a direction, follow through, and make the neces-sary corrections to stay on track.
- ☐ You prioritize your life and tasks, and then take action.
- ☐ You set goals that keep you effective and efficient.
- ☐ You become frustrated when you when a group you are a part of doesn't have clear goals or direction. Likewise, your life and work become frustrating when your goals are unclear.

The genius of Focus talents is in your intense concentration on one task. Your single-mindedness enhances the speed and quality of your performance.

Futuristic as One of Your Signature Themes

To begin affirming Futuristic as one of your areas of dominant talents, first take another look at the description of that theme:

"Wouldn't it be great if . . ." You are the kind of person who loves to peer over the horizon. The future fascinates you. As if it were projected on the wall, you see in detail what the future might hold, and this detailed picture keeps pulling you forward, into tomorrow. While the exact content of the picture will depend on your other strengths and interests — a better product, a better team, a better life, or a better world — it will always be inspirational to you. You are a dreamer who sees visions of what could be and who cherishes those visions. When the present proves too frustrating and the people around you too pragmatic, you conjure up your visions of the future and they energize you. They can energize others, too. In fact, very often people look to you to describe your visions of the future. They want a picture that can raise their sights and thereby their spirits. You can paint it for them. Practice. Choose your words carefully. Make the picture as vivid as possible. People will want to latch on to the hope you bring.

Now, consider this statement based on comments from individuals who possess Futuristic among their Signature Themes. It represents what Futuristic could "sound like."

"I'm only a freshman, but I'm anxious to decide whether to major in transportation planning or international business. Either way, I'll be prepared for what lies ahead. Of course, some of the jobs I'll have in life haven't even been invented yet!"

For further understanding of your talents, examine these insights and select those that describe you best.

- ☐ You are fascinated by the future, and you usually see the future positively.

- ☐ You can see in detail what the future might hold.

- ☐ You can energize yourself and others by your vision of what could be. You can clearly see possibilities.

☐ Others may dismiss you as a dreamer. You might become frustrated by present circumstances and discouraged by highly pragmatic people who can't or won't see the possible future that is so clear to you.

The genius of Futuristic talents is in your emotional anticipation and visual imagination of a better future, which inspire you — and could inspire others — to make that dream a reality.

Harmony as One of Your Signature Themes

To begin affirming Harmony as one of your areas of dominant talents, first take another look at the description of that theme:

You look for areas of agreement. In your view there is little to be gained from conflict and friction, so you seek to hold them to a minimum. When you know that the people around you hold differing views, you try to find the common ground. You try to steer them away from confrontation and toward harmony. In fact, harmony is one of your guiding values. You can't quite believe how much time is wasted by people trying to impose their views on others. Wouldn't we all be more productive if we kept our opinions in check and instead looked for consensus and support? You believe we would, and you live by that belief. When others are sounding off about their goals, their claims, and their fervently held opinions, you hold your peace. When others strike out in a direction, you will willingly, in the service of harmony, modify your own objectives to merge with theirs (as long as their basic values do not clash with yours). When others start to argue about their pet theory or concept, you steer clear of the debate, preferring to talk about practical, down-to-earth matters on which you can all agree. In your view we are all in the same boat, and we need this boat to get where we are going. It is a good boat. There is no need to rock it just to show that you can.

Now, consider this statement based on comments from individuals who possess Harmony among their Signature Themes. It represents what Harmony could "sound like."

"In my family I'm known as the peacemaker. Somehow I'm able to work behind the scenes to help resolve or even prevent conflicts. Half the time, the people involved don't realize all the conversations I've had with both sides to help them reach a win-win solution."

For further understanding of your talents, examine these insights and select those that describe you best.

☐ You want peace, and you try to bring people together.

☐ You can see points that people have in common, even when they are in conflict.

☐ You seek to help individuals, families, and organizations work together.

☐ Some people may criticize you, saying you lack courage. Occasionally, even you may see your desire for harmony as an avoidance of conflict.

The genius of Harmony talents is in your natural practicality and preference for emotional efficiency. By reducing friction, you enhance collaboration.

Ideation as One of Your Signature Themes

To begin affirming Ideation as one of your areas of dominant talents, first take another look at the description of that theme:

You are fascinated by ideas. What is an idea? An idea is a concept, the best explanation of the most events. You are delighted when you discover beneath the complex surface an elegantly simple concept to explain why things are the way they are. An idea is a connection. Yours is the kind of mind that is always looking for connections, and so you are intrigued when seemingly disparate phenomena can be linked by an obscure connection. An idea is a new perspective on familiar challenges. You revel in taking the world we all know and turning it around so we can view it from a strange but strangely enlightening angle. You love all these ideas because they are profound, because they are novel, because they are clarifying, because they are contrary, because they are bizarre.

For all these reasons you derive a jolt of energy whenever a new idea occurs to you. Others may label you creative or original or conceptual or even smart. Perhaps you are all of these. Who can be sure? What you are sure of is that ideas are thrilling. And on most days this is enough.

Now, consider this statement based on comments from individuals who possess Ideation among their Signature Themes. It represents what Ideation could "sound like."

"In my psychology class, we were supposed to do a group research project on mental illness. Every other group presented a report to the class, but I talked my group into making a creative video about what it might be like to experience mental illness. All the research was there — it was just presented in a really cool way that helped everybody remember it better."

For further understanding of your talents, examine these insights and select those that describe you best.

- ☐ You are a creative person, and you appreciate originality.
- ☐ You like free-thinking experiences such as brainstorming and discussion groups.
- ☐ You love new ideas and concepts.
- ☐ At times, it may seem like you get lost in the world of ideas, and others may think you are a daydreamer.

The genius of Ideation talents is in your spontaneous creativity. You have a natural sense of innovation that can defy conventional thinking.

Includer as One of Your Signature Themes

To begin affirming Includer as one of your areas of dominant talents, first take another look at the description of that theme:

"Stretch the circle wider." This is the philosophy around which you orient your life. You want to include people and make them feel part of the group. In direct contrast to those who are drawn only to exclusive groups, you actively avoid those groups that exclude others. You want to expand the group so that as many people as possible can benefit from its support. You hate the sight of someone on the outside looking in. You want to draw them in so that they can feel the warmth of the group. You are an instinctively accepting person. Regardless of race or sex or nationality or personality or faith, you cast few judgments. Judgments can hurt a person's feelings. Why do that if you don't have to? Your accepting nature does not necessarily rest on a belief that each of us is different and that one should respect these differences. Rather, it rests on your conviction that fundamentally we are all the same. We are all equally important. Thus, no one should be ignored. Each of us should be included. It is the least we all deserve.

Now, consider this statement based on comments from individuals who possess Includer among their Signature Themes. It represents what Includer could "sound like."

"In class, I noticed one guy who always ended up by himself when the professor would tell us to get into groups. I could tell he was feeling left out, so I invited him to join our group."

For further understanding of your talents, examine these insights and select those that describe you best.

☐ You notice people who feel like outsiders or who feel unappreciated.

☐ You are not content when people are left out, so you try to reach out to the "outsiders" and bring them in.

☐ People see you as accepting and sense that you want them to be included.

☐ In your attempts to include others, you may be rejected by the very people you try to include. You may have to confront your own fears as you seek to include those who may reject you. You may also have to deal with people who misunderstand your actions, yet themselves do nothing to reach out to those who feel left out.

The genius of Includer talents lies in your sensitivity to those who are excluded and your desire and capacity to bring them into the group.

Individualization as One of Your Signature Themes

To begin affirming Individualization as one of your areas of dominant talents, first take another look at the description of that theme:

Your Individualization theme leads you to be intrigued by the unique qualities of each person. You are impatient with generalizations or "types" because you don't want to obscure what is special and distinct about each person. Instead, you focus on the differences between individuals. You instinctively observe each person's style, each person's motivation, how each thinks, and how each builds relationships. You hear the one-of-a-kind stories in each person's life. This theme explains why you pick your friends just the right birthday gift, why you know that one person prefers praise in public and another detests it, and why you tailor your teaching style to accommodate one person's need to be shown and another's desire to "figure it out as I go." Because you are such a keen observer of other people's strengths, you can draw out the best in each person. This Individualization theme also helps you build productive teams. While some search around for the perfect team "structure" or "process," you know instinctively that the secret to great teams is casting by individual strengths so that everyone can do a lot of what they do well.

Now, consider this statement based on comments from individuals who possess Individualization among their Signature Themes. It represents what Individualization could "sound like."

"I'm coaching an after-school youth basketball team at the YMCA. It's cool to see what brings out the best in each of my players. Tony responds really well when I match him up on defense with the top player on the other team; Jay gets into it most when I tell him he's NBA material. And Daniel shines when I keep track of how many steals he has in a game and make a big deal of that."

For further understanding of your talents, examine these insights and select those that describe you best.

☐ You view each person as a distinct, one-of-a-kind individual.

☐ You naturally see how people who are very different can work together well.

☐ You know how to build productive teams because you can see the talents of people and structure groups that maximize those talents.

☐ Because you see individuals so distinctly and try to relate to them in terms of their specific characteristics, relating to people can be sometimes be tiring and even overwhelming.

The genius of Individualization talents is in your ability to notice and appreciate the unique characteristics of each person, and to customize your approach accordingly.

Input as One of Your Signature Themes

To begin affirming Input as one of your areas of dominant talents, first take another look at the description of that theme:

You are inquisitive. You collect things. You might collect information — words, facts, books, and quotations — or you might collect tangible objects such as butterflies, baseball cards, porcelain dolls, or sepia photographs. Whatever you collect, you collect it because it interests you. And yours is the kind of mind that finds so many things interesting. The world is exciting precisely because of its infinite variety and complexity. If you read a great deal, it is not necessarily to refine your theories but, rather, to add more information to your archives. If you like to travel, it is because each new location offers novel artifacts and facts. These can be acquired and then stored away. Why are they worth storing? At the time of storing it is often hard to say exactly when or why you might need them, but who knows when they might become useful? With all those possible uses in mind, you really don't feel comfortable throwing anything away. So you keep acquiring and compiling and filing stuff away. It's interesting. It keeps your mind fresh. And perhaps one day some of it will prove valuable.

Now, consider this statement based on comments from individuals who possess Input among their Signature Themes. It represents what Input could "sound like."

"When I go on the Internet to do research for a paper, I can easily find relevant and appropriate information that help me get the paper written. In fact, I often find extra information that will help my friends get their papers written, too."

For further understanding of your talents, examine these insights and select those that describe you best.

- ☐ You always want to know more. You crave information.
- ☐ You like to collect certain things, such as ideas, books, memorabilia, quotations, and facts.
- ☐ You have an active curiosity. You find many things very interesting. A few minutes of "surfing the Net" may turn into hours once your curiosity takes off, and you might have difficulties filing and housing all of the new information you acquire.

The genius of Input talents is in your active and resourceful curiosity, which leads you to become a storehouse of knowledge.

Intellection as One of Your Signature Themes

To begin affirming Intellection as one of your areas of dominant talents, first take another look at the description of that theme:

You like to think. You like mental activity. You like exercising the "muscles" of your brain, stretching them in multiple directions. This need for mental activity may be focused; for example, you may be trying to solve a problem or develop an idea or understand another person's feelings. The exact focus will depend on your other strengths. On the other hand, this mental activity may very well lack focus. The theme of Intellection does not dictate what you are thinking about; it simply describes that you like to think. You are the kind of person who enjoys your time alone because it is your time for musing and reflection. You are introspective. In a sense you are your own best companion, as you pose yourself questions and try out answers on yourself to see how they sound. This introspection may lead you to a slight sense of discontent as you compare what you are actually doing with all the thoughts and ideas that your mind conceives. Or this introspection may tend toward more pragmatic matters such as the events of the day or a conversation that you plan to have later. Wherever it leads you, this mental hum is one of the constants of your life.

Now, consider this statement based on comments from individuals who possess Intellection among their Signature Themes. It represents what Intellection could "sound like."

"I once got to house-sit for one of my professors. The time away from all the noise and activity at the dorm was a great opportunity to think about the best way to approach the rest of the semester."

For further understanding of your talents, examine these insights and select those that describe you best.

☐ You love to study, and you prefer intellectual discussions.

☐ You like to think and to let your thoughts go in many directions.

☐ You like to spend time alone so that you can reflect and ponder.

☐ Others may write you off as a "geek" because of your sophisticated level of thinking and use of language.

The genius of Intellection talents stems from the deep processing that occurs when you think. Wisdom and clarity result from your ability to muse for long periods of time.

Learner as One of Your Signature Themes

To begin affirming Learner as one of your areas of dominant talents, first take another look at the description of that theme:

You love to learn. The subject matter that interests you most will be determined by your other themes and experiences, but whatever the subject, you will always be drawn to the process of learning. The process, more than the content or the result, is especially exciting for you. You are energized by the steady and deliberate journey from ignorance to competence. The thrill of the first few facts, the early efforts to recite or practice what you have learned, the growing confidence of a skill mastered — this is the process that entices you. Your excitement leads you to engage in adult learning experiences — yoga or piano lessons or graduate classes. It enables you to thrive in dynamic work environments where you are asked to take on short project assignments and are expected to learn a lot about the new subject matter in a short period of time and then move on to the next one. This Learner theme does not necessarily mean that you seek to become the subject matter expert, or that you are striving for the respect that accompanies a professional or academic credential. The outcome of the learning is less significant than the "getting there."

Now, consider this statement based on comments from individuals who possess Learner among their Signature Themes. It represents what Learner could "sound like."

"I'm headed to Spain for a semester next year. I've been reading everything I can get my hands on about what it will be like to travel and live with a family in Seville."

For further understanding of your talents, examine these insights and select those that describe you best.

☐ You want to continuously learn and improve.

☐ You enjoy the process of learning as much as what you actually learn — perhaps even more.

☐ You get a thrill out of learning new facts, beginning a new subject, and mastering an important skill. Learning builds your confidence.

☐ You can get frustrated about wanting to learn so many different things because you fear you'll never be an expert.

The genius of Learner talents is that you not only love to learn; you also intuitively know how you learn best.

Maximizer as One of Your Signature Themes

To begin affirming Maximizer as one of your areas of dominant talents, first take another look at the description of that theme:

Excellence, not average, is your measure. Taking something from below average to slightly above average takes a great deal of effort and in your opinion is not very rewarding. Transforming something strong into something superb takes just as much effort but is much more thrilling. Strengths, whether yours or someone else's, fascinate you. Like a diver after pearls, you search them out, watching for the telltale signs of a strength. A glimpse of untutored excellence, rapid learning, a skill mastered without recourse to steps — all these are clues that a strength may be in play. And having found a strength, you feel compelled to nurture it, refine it, and stretch it toward excellence. You polish the pearl until it shines. This natural sorting of strengths means that others see you as discriminating. You choose to spend time with people who appreciate your particular strengths. Likewise, you are attracted to others who seem to have found and cultivated their own strengths. You tend to avoid those who want to fix you and make you well rounded. You don't want to spend your life bemoaning what you lack. Rather, you want to capitalize on the gifts with which you are blessed. It's more fun. It's more productive. And, counterintuitively, it is more demanding.

Now, consider this statement based on comments from individuals who possess Maximizer among their Signature Themes. It represents what Maximizer could "sound like."

"I was elected to student government and am heading a committee for our big Celebrate Diversity event on campus. I keep seeing ways we can make the event even better than it was last year, even though the rest of the committee thinks what we're doing so far is good enough."

For further understanding of your talents, examine these insights and select those that describe you best.

☐ You see talents and strengths in others, sometimes before they do.

☐ You love to help others become excited by the natural potential of their talents.

☐ You have the capacity to see what people will do best and which jobs they will be good at. You can see how people's talents match the tasks that must be completed.

☐ Some people may see you as picky or plodding because they don't understand your exceptional commitment to excellence.

The genius of Maximizer talents is in your natural discrimination toward better and your preference for working with and toward the best.

Positivity as One of Your Signature Themes

To begin affirming Positivity as one of your areas of dominant talents, first take another look at the description of that theme:

You are generous with praise, quick to smile, and always on the lookout for the positive in the situation. Some call you lighthearted. Others just wish that their glass were as full as yours seems to be. But either way, people want to be around you. Their world looks better around you because your enthusiasm is contagious. Lacking your energy and optimism, some find their world drab with repetition or, worse, heavy with pressure. You seem to find a way to lighten their spirit. You inject drama into every project. You celebrate every achievement. You find ways to make every- thing more exciting and more vital. Some cynics may reject your energy, but you are rarely dragged down. Your Positivity won't allow it. Somehow you can't quite escape your conviction that it is good to be alive, that work can be fun, and that no matter what the setbacks, one must never lose one's sense of humor.

Now, consider this statement based on comments from individuals who possess Positivity among their Signature Themes. It represents what Positivity could "sound like."

"College is great! There are lots of assignments and it's hard work, but it's such a fun and energizing atmosphere. Even when I'm buried in homework, I can't help but have a good time."

For further understanding of your talents, examine these insights and select those that describe you best.

☐ You bring enthusiasm to people, groups, and organizations.

☐ You can stimulate people to be more productive and become more hopeful.

☐ You can get people excited about what they are doing, causing them to become more engaged in their work.

☐ Some people will criticize you for being so optimistic. They may say you are naïve, and that may cause you to doubt yourself.

The genius of Positivity talents is found in your positive emotional impact. Simply stated, everyone feels better about life when you are around.

Relator as One of Your Signature Themes

To begin affirming Relator as one of your areas of dominant talents, first take another look at the description of that theme:

Relator describes your attitude toward your relationships. In simple terms, the Relator theme pulls you toward people you already know. You do not necessarily shy away from meeting new people — in fact, you may have other themes that cause you to enjoy the thrill of turning strangers into friends — but you do derive a great deal of pleasure and strength from being around your close friends. You are comfortable with intimacy. Once the initial connection has been made, you deliberately encourage a deepening of the relationship. You want to understand their feelings, their goals, their fears, and their dreams; and you want them to understand yours. You know that this kind of closeness implies a certain amount of risk — you might be taken advantage of — but you are willing to accept that risk. For you a relationship has value only if it is genuine. And the only way to know that is to entrust yourself to the other person. The more you share with each other, the more you risk together. The more you risk together, the more each of you proves your caring is genuine. These are your steps toward real friendship, and you take them willingly.

Now, consider this statement based on comments from individuals who possess Relator among their Signature Themes. It represents what Relator could "sound like."

"Leaving all my high school friends behind when I started college was hard. Even though I'm meeting a bunch of people here, there's such a big difference between being friendly with people and actually being friends."

For further understanding of your talents, examine these insights and select those that describe you best.

☐ You can form close relationships with people, and you enjoy doing so.

☐ You receive profound satisfaction from working hard with friends to accomplish an important goal.

☐ You know many people, and you can relate with all kinds of people. But you also have a very small group of friends with whom you have incredibly deep relationships.

☐ Some people may feel threatened or uncomfortable because they don't have the close, intense personal relationships that you thrive on.

The genius of Relator talents is in your ability to form solid, mutually rewarding relationships.

Responsibility as One of Your Signature Themes

To begin affirming Responsibility as one of your areas of dominant talents, first take another look at the description of that theme:

Your Responsibility theme forces you to take psychological ownership for anything you commit to, and whether large or small, you feel emotionally bound to follow it through to completion. Your good name depends on it. If for some reason you cannot deliver, you automatically start to look for ways to make it up to the other person. Apologies are not enough. Excuses and rationalizations are totally unacceptable. You will not quite be able to live with yourself until you have made restitution. This conscientiousness, this near obsession for doing things right, and your impeccable ethics, combine to create your reputation: utterly dependable. When assigning new responsibilities, people will look to you first because they know it will get done. When people come to you for help — and they soon will — you must be selective. Your willingness to volunteer may sometimes lead you to take on more than you should.

Now, consider this statement based on comments from individuals who possess Responsibility among their Signature Themes. It represents what Responsibility could "sound like."

"I'm not always thrilled about group projects when the professor assigns the groups. I just don't want to get stuck with someone who doesn't pull their weight or do quality work. If I'm going to partner with someone, I want them to deliver — just like I always do."

For further understanding of your talents, examine these insights and select those that describe you best.

☐ You are dependable, and people know it. They count on you when something important is on the line.

☐ You don't want to let people down, and you will work very hard to fulfill all your responsibilities and keep your word.

☐ Because you "come through" for people, word spreads — and more and more people come to you.

☐ With the responsibility you feel to the people who come to you and with the demands that each of them brings, you might feel overwhelmed and under pressure to perform.

The genius of Responsibility talents stems from the deep commitments you make to others and the ownership you feel. Because you are a person of your word, people trust you and count on you.

Restorative as One of Your Signature Themes

To begin affirming Restorative as one of your areas of dominant talents, first take another look at the description of that theme:

You love to solve problems. Whereas some are dismayed when they encounter yet another breakdown, you can be energized by it. You enjoy the challenge of analyzing the symptoms, identifying what is wrong, and finding the solution. You may prefer practical problems or conceptual ones or personal ones. You may seek out specific kinds of problems that you have met many times before and that you are confident you can fix. Or you may feel the greatest push when faced with complex and unfamiliar problems. Your exact preferences are determined by your other themes and experiences. But what is certain is that you enjoy bringing things back to life. It is a wonderful feeling to identify the undermining factor(s), eradicate them, and restore something to its true glory. Intuitively, you know that without your intervention, this thing — this machine, this technique, this person, this company — might have ceased to function. You fixed it, resuscitated it, rekindled its vitality. Phrasing it the way you might, you saved it.

Now, consider this statement based on comments from individuals who possess Restorative among their Signature Themes. It represents what Restorative could "sound like."

"I'm loving my business ethics class right now. We're doing case studies where we get to analyze all the problems in a company and figure out how to make the best decision. My prof tells me I'm really good at finding all the flaws and fixing them."

For further understanding of your talents, examine these insights and select those that describe you best.

- ☐ You readily take on projects that others believe "can't be saved."
- ☐ You can analyze a situation and identify potential shortcomings and what needs to be fixed.
- ☐ You quickly recognize problems that others may not detect.

☐ Other people may not like the fact that you can so quickly determine the problems and weaknesses in people, situations, and organizations. They may find this embarrassing, even if your assessments and solutions are accurate.

The genius of Restorative talents is in your love of problems. While others shy away, your solution-oriented mind naturally gravitates toward these challenges.

Self-Assurance as One of Your Signature Themes

To begin affirming Self-Assurance as one of your areas of dominant talents, first take another look at the description of that theme:

Self-Assurance is similar to self-confidence. In the deepest part of you, you have faith in your strengths. You know that you are able — able to take risks, able to meet new challenges, able to stake claims, and, most important, able to deliver. But Self-Assurance is more than just self-confidence. Blessed with the theme of Self-Assurance, you have confidence not only in your abilities but in your judgment. When you look at the world, you know that your perspective is unique and distinct. And because no one sees exactly what you see, you know that no one can make your decisions for you. No one can tell you what to think. They can guide. They can suggest. But you alone have the authority to form conclusions, make decisions, and act. This authority, this final accountability for the living of your life, does not intimidate you. On the contrary, it feels natural to you. No matter what the situation, you seem to know what the right decision is. This theme lends you an aura of certainty. Unlike many, you are not easily swayed by someone else's arguments, no matter how persuasive they may be. This Self-Assurance may be quiet or loud, depending on your other themes, but it is solid. It is strong. Like the keel of a ship, it withstands many different pressures and keeps you on your course.

Now, consider this statement based on comments from individuals who possess Self-Assurance among their Signature Themes. It represents what Self-Assurance could "sound like."

"I wasn't recruited to play baseball here, but I'm trying out as a walk-on. I know I can make it — I feel it in my gut as I practice with the others. I can do this!"

For further understanding of your talents, examine these insights and select those that describe you best.

☐ You are confident about your ability to manage your life.

☐ You can "bounce back" from disappointments and crises.

☐ You believe that your decisions are right and that your perspective is unique and distinct.

☐ Other people may see your self-assurance as a type of pride or arrogance. They might think you're cocky and not care for the way you tend to trust your own gut rather than others' advice.

The genius of Self-Assurance talents is in the way you deeply trust your own instincts. This can enable you to forge ahead confidently, even on risky paths.

Significance as One of Your Signature Themes

To begin affirming Significance as one of your areas of dominant talents, first take another look at the description of that theme:

You want to be very significant in the eyes of other people. In the truest sense of the word you want to be recognized. You want to be heard. You want to stand out. You want to be known. In particular, you want to be known and appreciated for the unique strengths you bring. You feel a need to be admired as credible, professional, and successful. Likewise, you want to associate with others who are credible, professional, and successful. And if they aren't, you will push them to achieve until they are. Or you will move on. An independent spirit, you want your work to be a way of life rather than a job, and in that work you want to be given free rein, the leeway to do things your way. Your yearnings feel intense to you, and you honor those yearnings. And so your life is filled with goals, achievements, or qualifications that you crave. Whatever your focus — and each person is distinct — your Significance theme will keep pulling you upward, away from the mediocre toward the exceptional. It is the theme that keeps you reaching.

Now, consider this statement based on comments from individuals who possess Significance among their Signature Themes. It represents what Significance could "sound like."

"One of my favorite high school memories is winning the 'servant leader' award for the work I did with inner-city kids in after-school programs. Knowing that people noticed the work I had done felt really good, especially when I knew I had made a difference in the lives of those kids."

For further understanding of your talents, examine these insights and select those that describe you best.

☐ You probably enjoy receiving public recognition for the differences you make.

☐ You want to have an impact on other people, groups, and society as a whole.

☐ You want the contributions you make to be viewed as substantial, powerful, and significant.

☐ Significance talents are sometimes perceived as egotism or a need for attention.

The genius of Significance talents begins and ends with the difference you are determined to make. You want the world to be a better place because you are in it.

Strategic as One of Your Signature Themes

To begin affirming Strategic as one of your areas of dominant talents, first take another look at the description of that theme:

The Strategic theme enables you to sort through the clutter and find the best route. It is not a skill that can be taught. It is a distinct way of thinking, a special perspective on the world at large. This perspective allows you to see patterns where others simply see complexity. Mindful of these patterns, you play out alternative scenarios, always asking, "What if this happened? Okay, well what if this happened?" This recurring question helps you see around the next corner. There you can evaluate accurately the potential obstacles. Guided by where you see each path leading, you start to make selections. You discard the paths that lead nowhere. You discard the paths that lead straight into resistance. You discard the paths that lead into a fog of confusion. You cull and make selections until you arrive at the chosen path — your strategy. Armed with your strategy, you strike forward. This is your Strategic theme at work: "What if?" Select. Strike.

Now, consider this statement based on comments from individuals who possess Strategic among their Signature Themes. It represents what Strategic could "sound like."

"I chose this college to prepare for medical school. I'd like to do it as quickly as possible, so I considered trying to finish in three years. But I want to get into a top school, so I'm going to limit the credit hours I take each semester and get really good grades."

For further understanding of your talents, examine these insights and select those that describe you best.

☐ You know that there is more than one means to an end. Your ability to see options helps you quickly come up with Plan B if your first plan doesn't work.

☐ You can quickly pick out the relevant issues and patterns when confronted by problems and complexities.

☐ You have a "What if this happens?" mentality toward work and life. This type of questioning helps you see, plan, and prepare for future situations.

☐ Some may see your lightning-quick evaluation of what won't work as overly critical. Because you are able to sort through everything so quickly, people don't realize that you have considered all the options.

The genius of Strategic talents is found in your ability to quickly weigh various alternative paths and determine the one that will work best and most efficiently. Sometimes you think backwards — visualizing the outcome you want and then generating multiple ways of reaching that goal.

Woo as One of Your Signature Themes

To begin affirming Woo as one of your areas of dominant talents, first take another look at the description of that theme:

Woo stands for winning others over. You enjoy the challenge of meeting new people and getting them to like you. Strangers are rarely intimidating to you. On the contrary, strangers can be energizing. You are drawn to them. You want to learn their names, ask them questions, and find some area of common interest so that you can strike up a conversation and build rapport. Some people shy away from starting up conversations because they worry about running out of things to say. You don't. Not only are you rarely at a loss for words; you actually enjoy initiating with strangers because you derive satisfaction from breaking the ice and making a connection. Once that connection is made, you are quite happy to wrap it up and move on. There are new people to meet, new rooms to work, new crowds to mingle in. In your world there are no strangers, only friends you haven't met yet — lots of them.

Now, consider this statement based on comments from individuals who possess Woo among their Signature Themes. It represents what Woo could "sound like."

"The first day of classes is always so fun. I made a lot of new friends today and introduced myself to each of my professors!"

For further understanding of your talents, examine these insights and select those that describe you best.

☐ You have the capacity to quickly connect with people and generate positive responses from them.

☐ You can enter a crowd of people and easily know what to do and what to say.

☐ You see no strangers — only friends you haven't met yet.

☐ Because you know so many people, some may believe that you form only shallow relationships. Others, however, will envy how quickly and easily you make friends.

The genius of Woo talents is in your ability to quickly connect with people and become a catalyst in helping them connect with one another. You have an exceptional sense of how to draw others out.

Chapter IV

RELATIONSHIPS FROM
THE STRENGTHS PERSPECTIVE

When we first began to talk to college students about strengths, an interesting thing happened. All along we had been focusing on how discovering talents and developing strengths could lead to excellence in terms of academic success in college. Our research had shown that this was indeed happening. But when we talked to students who had been through some of the earliest strengths-development programs with us, they always began by telling us how it had affected their relationships with others. A word that kept coming up in their conversations was "see."

Students told us that as a result of focusing on talents — the foundation of strengths — they were seeing themselves in a new way, as individuals with powerful talents in particular areas. Qualities that they'd been forever teased about or criticized for were seen from a different angle — as their greatest talents and their potential for strengths.

They told us they saw others differently as well — in light of *their* talents. Behaviors that used to annoy or irritate them simply because they were unfamiliar were seen from a different perspective and recognized as talents that could lead to excellence. Conflicts with others that previously had been viewed as crises or disasters were now regarded as opportunities to find common ground, because they realized they now had a new way of understanding others who were different from themselves.

We were thrilled! This new way of seeing things was a bonus, an unexpected finding. Psychologists have always emphasized that seeing things from a different perspective — what is sometimes called "reframing" — could help resolve conflicts and improve relationships. We knew this could be a powerful insight for students.

Chip Anderson, one of the authors of this book, took this insight and decided to apply it in a compelling way. We were gathered at a large conference for college faculty and staff. In walked Chip, larger than life, carrying sacks of colorful plastic glasses. As he handed them out to everyone in the room, he shared insights about how becoming aware of one's talents and seeing the areas of greatest talent in others could lead to dramatic changes in relationships. He challenged all of us to see our students through "strengths-colored glasses" and discover for ourselves how this would change and enrich our interactions with them and our ways of educating them.

Sadly, Chip died in July of 2005. At his funeral, some of the educators who had attended this conference brought those same plastic glasses with them. They told others how that simple visual image had been a turning point for them both professionally and personally.

So imagine you have in your hands a new pair of glasses. Put them on for a while and see how your world changes.

The Lenses of Reality

Part of being human is having a lens through which we view reality. An old Chinese proverb states, "Two thirds of what we see is behind our eyes." Our family of origin and our culture have crafted these lenses to a certain extent, as have our own experiences and thoughts. Our lenses determine how we emotionally respond to an event; the same incident can happen to two people who interpret it very differently, leading them to respond differently as well.

For example: Jake, Mike, and Tim are buddies who are supposed to meet at the local coffee house to work on a class project. Jake and Tim are there on time, but Mike is 30 minutes late. Jake shrugs it off — after all, who knows the things that might have come up at the last minute? But Tim, who sees through different lenses, is fuming. He's frustrated and angry at what he sees as Mike's lack of consideration.

Now take the situation and heighten the sensitivities and even prejudices. When we don't know someone very well and the person is different from us, we may tend to jump to some conclusions about him or her based on what we *can* see — general appearance, hairstyle, accent, demeanor, race, or gender. So suppose Mike is someone from class who has been assigned to a group project with Jake and Tim. Mike commutes from off-campus because he has a part-time job and can't afford to live in the residence hall; also, he was born and raised in a "sleepy" rural town. Mike is 30 minutes late and saunters into the coffee house, sliding casually into a comfortable position on the nearest couch. How will Jake's and Tim's lenses interpret what they see? What prejudicial conclusions might they draw about Mike's commitment to the group project?

Now, suppose for a minute that in the same class the professor had taken the time to explain to students how talents affect relationships. Further, suppose the professor had designed some group exercises that would help the students get to know one another and figure out how they could best use their talents to work together. With those talent insights in mind, when Mike slides onto the couch 30 minutes late, Jake and Tim are laughing good-naturedly. That's because two of Mike's Signature Themes are Adaptability and Input. Not uncharacteristically, Mike had lost track of time while his Input talents drove him to surf the Internet for in-depth and comprehensive research for the group project. Jake and Tim were eager to hear about what he had found.

Seeing Differently

There are three ways that we see people's vision changing when they wear strengths-colored glasses: (1) they see themselves differently, (2) they see their futures differently, and (3) they see others differently.

Seeing Yourself Differently

We each have a view of ourselves that has developed since early in life. This view, known as our self-concept, is how we answer the question "Who am I?" In many ways, it determines the lens through which we view others and the world as a whole. When our self-concept is mostly negative, we tend to see others negatively as well and view the world pessimistically. When our self-concept is mostly positive, we give others the benefit of the doubt, are more optimistic about the future and the world, and enjoy more positive relationships. As the author Anais Nin has said, "We don't see things as they are. We see them as *we* are."

Self-concept is a combination of what other people have told us about ourselves, what we have discovered about ourselves through our experiences of success and failure, what we've learned about ourselves as we compare ourselves to others, and what our culture has told us about ourselves. We are bombarded with advertising that encourages us to compare ourselves to others who are prettier, smarter, more athletic, make more money, or are with someone more attractive. Too often the focus is on who you *aren't* rather than on who you are. This focus on "not enough" is meant to get us to buy things, but it has the side effect of shaping our view of ourselves and the lens through which we view others.

The Impact of Culture on Self-Concept

Our culture contributes to our self-concept by sending us messages about what is most valued by others in the culture and by providing role models. Some cultures emphasize independence, being your own person, and making your own way, while others stress your connections to others and what you contribute to your family or to society. These become lenses through which you view yourself and others, and by which you make judgments about those who are different.

When you learn to take a strengths approach to life, you see yourself through a different set of lenses. Where you once focused on all the things you couldn't do as well as someone else, you now see that there are areas of talent within you that have always been there and that flourish best in certain kinds of environments. Where before you might have been afraid to try new things, now you realize that you are capable of succeeding in your areas of greatest talent — so you have the courage to rise to the occasion as you recognize where your talents are needed. As a result, we've found that college students who are aware of their most powerful talents and who learn how to develop strengths become much more self-confident, which in turn provides the motivation to take on new challenges and achieve excellence.

Self-Knowledge and Self-Acceptance

The foundation of mental health is self-knowledge and self-acceptance: knowing who you are and being okay with that. Healthy relationships depend on being comfortable enough with yourself that you are able to share yourself with another person. Optimal functioning — getting the most out of your life — starts with a realistic awareness of who you are and what you have to offer others. "Love your neighbor as yourself," a value that is common to many faith traditions, is built on the assumption that you cannot love someone else until you love yourself — not in an egotistical, self-absorbed way, but genuinely appreciating who you are inside your own skin. That's where it all starts.

Self-awareness means you see your talents and strengths clearly, but it also means you are aware of your weaknesses. By weaknesses we simply mean *any lack of knowledge, skill, or talent that negatively affects your performance or that of others.* Note that areas of lesser talent are not the same as weaknesses. For example, a doctor who can't carry a tune does not have a weakness; she just has lesser talent in singing. But if that same doctor possesses lesser talents in communicating, that's a weakness — it interferes with her ability to effectively communicate with her patients.

Weaknesses can't be ignored, because they prevent you or another person from performing with strength. Focusing on building strengths does not mean your weaknesses no longer matter. The difference is that you now see these weaknesses as obstacles to be managed, skills to be learned, or knowledge to be acquired. A large part of the secret of success in life is learning to apply your areas of greatest talent to manage your weaknesses.

Here's an example: Suppose the same doctor recognizes that her lack of clear communication with her patients hampers her effectiveness as a physician. She can manage this weakness in any number of ways. One way is to partner with someone else; she could choose to hire an outstanding empathic communicator as a personal assistant who is always in the room with her when she needs to talk to her patients. This partnership is not particularly cost-effective, but it is one way to proactively manage the weakness.

The second option is to recognize that though consistently near-perfect communication requires exceptional communication talents, skills can be learned, allowing the doctor to at least improve her communication.

This doctor, whose greatest talents happen to be in the Strategic and Analytical themes, weighs the evidence and realizes that effectively communicating with her patients is crucial to helping them heal quickly. So she learns some basic communication skills and asks her head nurse, a somewhat more talented communicator, to follow up with all her patients to ensure that they have understood her instructions to them

This doctor has used her Strategic and Analytical talents to see that there is a problem, and to recognize that she must keep clear communication at the forefront of her mind because it will help her be more effective. Will she ever be a world-class communicator — communicating at the level of strength? Probably not. But she can learn to strategically manage her relationships with patients and become a more effective doctor by gaining some fundamental communication skills.

This whole process of learning about yourself, of becoming more self-aware, is a key task during the college years. It's one that takes a while to master. Benjamin Franklin once said, "There are three things extremely hard: steel, a diamond, and to know one's self." In our research with college students, we've found that those who like learning about themselves are those who gain the most from a strengths approach to their education and their relationships. When you start seeing yourself as possessing natural and exceptional talents, you realize you are already on the way toward achieving your goals.

Seeing Your Future Differently

Once you see yourself differently — as a person with valuable talents — you also begin to see your future differently. Hazel Markus, a psychologist at Stanford University, refers to the concept of "possible selves," which are ideas you have about what you might become in the future. Her research shows that having this vision of what one can become motivates students to set and achieve goals.

Students who view themselves from a strengths perspective see many possible selves that they could become. Markus and her colleagues have demonstrated that programs that help students see these possible selves lead to higher grades and a greater likelihood of graduating from college.

This vision for the future generates hope. Rick Snyder and Shane Lopez, two psychologists at the University of Kansas, have studied hope in college students. They've found that the level of hope a student possesses predicts how well that student will do in college and how likely he or she is to graduate.

But hope doesn't just affect your grades and graduation chances; having a high level of hope also is related to better health, a stronger sense of purpose in life, higher self-esteem, and less depression. Snyder and Lopez also discovered that an awareness of your talents and strengths creates pathways that lead to hope. You're far more likely to feel hopeful about the future if you see yourself as possessing the talents to get there.

Seeing Others Differently

Not only do you start seeing yourself and your future differently as a result of strengths-colored glasses; you also see those around you differently. As you begin to think seriously about the unique constellation of talents that you have, you recognize that other people each have their own unique combination of talents as well. You begin to see them through a different lens. The things that used to annoy or irritate you are now seen as the very things that make the other person productive or successful.

This reframing may start with your roommate, if you live on campus, or with the people you share space with off campus. Learning to live with someone new, particularly someone who is a total stranger, can be challenging. The list of potential roommate gripes is long: One of you prefers to get up early to study, while the other is a night owl who likes to study very late at night. One is a neat freak; the other is the world's biggest slob. You may have differing needs for privacy, may prefer quiet or noise, and have different tastes in friends and music.

But when you start seeing your roommate through strengths-colored glasses, you learn that her greatest talents lie in the area of Discipline, for instance — which you previously saw only as her annoyingly compulsive neatness, her regular routine and schedule for everything, and the way she gets upset when you bring your friends into the room for a party during her scheduled study time. Now you realize that those talents are not only what enable her to make the grade as a pre-med major, but also could be of help to you as you are trying to juggle all the demands of your own schedule. You realize that by communicating clearly with her in advance about your plans, there really are very few remaining areas of conflict.

Not only do you view your roommate differently when you start seeing through strengths-colored glasses; you also start seeing your family differently. Mark Twain famously said, "When I was a boy of fourteen, my father was so ignorant I could hardly stand to have the old man around. But when I got to be twenty-one, I was astonished at how much he had learned in seven years." Seeing your parents differently will happen naturally in the college years. But seeing all members of your family differently will happen more quickly when you view them in light of their talents and strengths. By sharing with them your areas of greatest talent, they may begin relating to you differently as well.

We have worked with parents as part of the strengths approach to the first-year experience in colleges. Sometimes today's parents are labeled "helicopter parents" — they hover protectively around their son or daughter even when the child has left for college, often rushing to the rescue in inappropriate ways. We heard of one first-year student in Michigan who couldn't find the building where his first class was scheduled. He called his mother in Georgia on his cell phone and she downloaded a campus map off of the Internet, giving him directions until he found the classroom.

For helicopter parents, viewing their children as independent adults is a difficult task. But once they start seeing their son or daughter through the lens of strengths, they realize their child has talents that will enable him or her to survive in the world. One parent said to us, "My son has some abilities I never knew he had. He has powerful Developer talents: I used to see that as taking too long to finish things and taking too much time with people who were struggling. Now I see how many people he has helped and how much other students here enjoy having him around. He views life and the world differently than me; understanding this will help me support him as he launches out on his own."

Seeing the significant people in your life differently also extends to those you are interested in dating — or to whom you are already married. When you care about someone, you want to see them become all that they are capable of being. When you see someone as exceptionally talented in the Empathy or Relator theme, for instance, it's harder to objectify them — they are still physically attractive to you, but you begin to relate to them as a unique human being that you want to know and understand more fully.

Marriage researcher John Gottman has made headlines with his ability to accurately predict couples who are likely to divorce just by watching how they interact with one another for as little as 15 minutes. When he first started his research, he studied failed marriages to learn something about successful ones, assuming that happy marriages were simply the opposite of unhappy marriages.

Gottman knew that in unhappy marriages both partners tended to have distorted and negative views of each other; they were often highly critical of one another. So he assumed that in happy marriages each person saw the other "realistically" and accurately. But he was wrong! In studying the really happy marriages, he noticed an intriguing dynamic: The husband saw his wife as possessing more talents and strengths than she saw herself possessing — and vice versa. It was as if they were seeing each other through rose-colored glasses — or as we would say, through "strengths-colored" glasses.

This is why studying success makes so much more sense than studying failure. Gottman and his colleagues would've missed this important point about happy marriages if they were focused on only the unhappy ones.

Cleaning Your Glasses

When asked what makes life meaningful, most people mention satisfying relationships before anything else. Ed Diener, a psychologist who has studied well-being across dozens of different countries, has found that only one factor consistently predicted feelings of well-being in every country he studied: social relationships.

The quality of your life is directly related to the quality of your relationships. So here are some tips for *how to clean your glasses* and see things from a different perspective that will enable you to have more satisfying relationships with others for a lifetime. To help you remember the connection between these five tips and "seeing," we've started each tip with a "C." (Excuse the aural pun — one of us has Ideation as a Signature Theme!)

1. Connect.

Start by recognizing how important it is to your physical and mental health that you have solid relationships with others. Relationships matter — not just for those who are in a new environment or are lonely, but also for those who have worked at the same job for decades or have been married a long time. You are more productive at work, get sick less, and change jobs less often when you have solid relationships with your boss and co-workers. Research shows that as a student you'll miss fewer classes, learn more, and be more likely to graduate if you develop relationships with your professors, other students in your classes, and students in campus organizations.

> **With Professors.** Richard Light, a professor at Harvard University, was part of a team that interviewed hundreds of successful students. The best advice these students offered to new students was to get to know their professors. One of the many beneficial results of developing a relationship with at least one professor each semester is the possibility of eight or more letters of reference and connections to jobs and grad schools when graduation rolls around. But more importantly, seeing your professors as unique human beings — many of whom have some of their greatest talents in the Learner theme — can help you learn better. After you've spent time with your professors and have come to know them as unique humans beings whom

you respect, you'll feel more comfortable asking questions in class or going to their offices to discuss something that sparked your interest. You'll become more engaged in your own learning because you have a relationship with the people who are there to facilitate your learning.

Some of the newest brain research shows that learning involves both emotional and intellectual connections. When you connect learning to *who you are* and *who you are in relationship with,* the learning process becomes personal, which makes it not only more enjoyable but more efficient and effective. So find out what makes your professors tick — ask them what they enjoy most about their work. See them as the unique persons they are — with particular constellations of talents and ways of seeing the world. Think about how knowing them as individuals helps you to relate to them and learn more from them.

With Other Students. Being able to connect to others and work well together is one of the most prized abilities that employers are looking for in new hires, according to research conducted by the National Association of College Employers. Those who have learned how their talents interact with the talents of others and what brings out their best are in a better position to connect.

This interdependence is a hallmark of a mature person; there is the recognition that other people are necessary in order to produce excellence. Knowing you have similar areas of exceptional talent gives you common ground for connecting. For instance, if both you and someone you meet in class are particularly talented in the Achiever theme, you understand each other's need for goals and you appreciate each other's commitment to hard work.

But if one of you is highly talented in Achiever and the other's top theme is Arranger, you can also recognize the potential power of partnering with one another. You recognize that although you approach life differently when it comes to goal-setting and structure, you both have in common the fact that you respond well under stress. Working on a group project together, the achiever can keep the group on task and map out all the things that need to be done, while the arranger can deal with the unexpected things that happen at the last minute, juggling all the pieces to pull the project together and turn it in on time.

2. Communicate.

While we've pointed out that teamwork is highly prized by employers, organizations most desire people with the ability to communicate. Surveys of top executives in the world's best companies have shown that these high flyers believe their communication abilities were the number-one factor that led them to the top.

So what are the building blocks of good communication?

Respect. The foundation of communication is respect for the person with whom you are communicating. Seeing each person as unique and of value enables you to communicate on an equal footing. Researchers believe one of the most basic building blocks of effective communication is this ability to see the other person as unique and of value.

This respect for the other person means that the first step in good communication is listening. Stephen Covey, author of *The Seven Habits of Highly Effective People,* says, "If I were to summarize in one sentence the single most important principle I have learned in the field of interpersonal relations, it would be this: Seek first to understand, then to be understood."

Listening. Seeking first to understand — before making sure that the other person understands you — means that you listen more than you talk. Referring back to the survey of top executives, research shows that on a typical day the average executive spends 60% of his or her time listening to others. Active listening is the term that describes what good listening is all about. It doesn't mean you sit there silently; you are actively involved in trying to understand where the other person is coming from. You listen for the meaning and the emotion behind the words. You are able to put into your own words what you've heard them say, rather than rehearsing what you are going to say next.

The Chinese character for "listen" reflects their cultural view that listening is a whole-body experience. The character is a combination of the characters for ears, eyes, heart, and undivided attention. The next time you're in a conversation with someone, let the other person speak first, and with your whole body listen actively to what they have to say. Notice the nonverbal cues they give you — how her arms are crossed or his foot is tapping. Try to understand what the other person may be feeling — what the Native American culture sometimes refers to as "walking a moon in my neighbor's moccasins." Realize that other cultures may value certain types of communication differently; as a result, persons from some cultures may forcefully argue an issue with you, while those from other cultures may prefer to save face or avoid eye contact when conflict arises.

What You Say and How You Say It. Communication is not just about listening, though. It's also about what you say and how you say it. Because our brains seem to be wired to pick up negative cues more easily than positive ones — and we tend to interpret negative communication as evidence of people's "true character" — it isn't enough to learn positive communication habits. We also have to learn to avoid the negative ones. In the most successful relationships, the ratio of positive to negative statements that couples make to each other is 5:1, according to John Gottman. Marriage experts Clifford Notarius and Howard Markman say it more boldly: "One zinger will erase 20 acts of kindness."

Those zingers are part of a negative communication pattern that demonstrate a lack of respect for the other person — a belief that your needs are more important than theirs or that the other person is not your equal in some way. Gottman says that *criticism, hostility, defensiveness, and stonewalling (refusing to talk things out)* are deadly to relationships. In fact, he calls these behaviors "the four horsemen of the Apocalypse," because they are such harbingers of doom.

Positive Communication. So what do positive communication abilities look like, and how do they compare to the negative ones? It's not just refraining from criticism or hostility — although that's a good start that will keep you physically as well as emotionally healthy!

Positive communication involves sharing yourself and your feelings with another person. This self-disclosure is part of what author Harriet Lerner calls "the dance of intimacy." When you first get to know someone, each person tends to share something about themselves that is fairly superficial — where they're from, what their major is, or how many siblings they have. Then the dance begins; as each person shares something a little more meaningful about themselves, the other person reciprocates. One shares that they are a first-generation college student; the other shares that this is their first time they've been away from home for more than a week. Each person shares something a little more meaningful about themselves in proportion to what the other person shares.

Going too deep too soon can scare the other person. Somehow, communicating that you are a recovering addict when the other person has simply shared that he is a big fan of the Boston Red Sox can put an end to the conversation, and even to the budding relationship. But if you continue to share only superficially when the other person has started to share something a little more meaningful, that can also put an end to the conversation. That's why Lerner calls it a dance — the interaction is almost choreographed in steps that enable people to mirror one another and develop a deeper relationship while still feeling comfortable and secure.

Self-disclosure often happens most effectively when people talk to one another about their talents. For example, when someone with exceptional Intellection talents is able to explain how much he or she enjoys mulling things over, the person with powerful Communication talents realizes that what originally seemed like an awkward silence between them is really just the other person taking time to carefully think about an issue before talking about it. Suddenly the silence is seen as valuable and as an indication that there is thinking going on.

Validation. Positive communication also involves letting people know you have heard them and understand them — regardless of whether you agree with them. Validation is an important human requirement; we all need to know that we matter to someone else and that our opinions count. Effective communicators find common ground. They look for areas of agreement and search for win-win solutions to problems. They let others know they respect their opinions and care enough to stay in the conversation. Rather than trying to change the other person, they focus on understanding where the other person is coming from and what kind of solution will enable them to continue working together.

Knowing the Signature Themes of the other person can be helpful in this process. When you learn that your friend's greatest talents lie in the Restorative theme, for instance, you can affirm his or her terrific problem-solving abilities. You also know that their commitment to your relationship will be strong even if things are strained between you, because they love to "bring things back to life." They'll stay in the conversation with you, even though your friend's emphasis may be on the problems in your relationship and what it will take to fix them.

3. Collaborate.

Earlier we mentioned how important it is to make connections with other people. This is especially true when you are in a learning environment. And with the rapid pace of change in our society, virtually every environment has become a learning environment.

Cooperative Learning. Cooperative learning is one of the best ways to capitalize on talents and optimize your learning. It starts with the recognition that learning is not a one-way street — it's not about the professor transmitting knowledge to the student. Learning is more complex: Students learn from professors, but professors also learn from students, and students learn from each other. Particularly in a culture as diverse as ours, there is a richness of experience that each member of a class brings to the learning environment. When we are able to hear these different voices and learn of perspectives on the world that are different from our own, our brain power expands exponentially.

In essence, all learning starts with dissonance — a realization that something is not what you thought it was. When your brain tries to figure out what's different and how it might be related to what you already know, an amazing amount of learning occurs. When the recognition of those differences happens in the context of positive emotions, our capability expands even further. Barbara Fredrickson at the University of Michigan calls this the "broaden and build" theory. That is, positive emotions open people's receptivity to new ideas and result in greater levels of creativity and problem-solving. Learning about one another and seeing each other's talents and strengths typically creates positive emotions, which can then form the basis for a solid learning experience together.

Group Projects. When group projects operate from a strengths perspective, the first discussion is about the particular talents that each group member brings to the project. The process of doing the project is just as important as the final product. So the student with powerful talents in Focus or Analytical maps out the parts of the project, while the student particularly talented in Responsibility helps assign roles and deadlines. The student with exceptional Includer talents makes sure everyone is satisfied with the role they're assigned, and the student highly talented in Consistency makes sure everyone is doing an equal amount of work. The student with Discipline talents at the forefront ensures that the professor's instructions are being followed to the letter, and the student who leads with Ideation talents helps the group see the big picture and brainstorm all the ways the project could be done.

The result? As the research we've done clearly shows, groups perform more effectively and the final product is much better. When a classroom operates from a strengths perspective, the students are more engaged in their own learning and tend to get grades better than those earned by students in the same classes that are not taught with this insight.

Other Ways to Collaborate. Even if your professor doesn't organize the class in this manner, you can still use the strengths perspective to collaborate with others. If there are group projects, you can encourage your team to talk about their talents and what each person contributes to the project. You can create your own study groups outside of class, to capitalize on the diverse talents of others in your classes. You can collaborate with others in your clubs or athletic teams by focusing on what each member contributes to the group's overall success. Talking together about how your talents complement one another can lead to what is called "synergy" — the tremendous result that occurs when a group of people discover and maximize their talents as a team, rather than simply contribute their talents as separate individuals. Something different and better happens when everyone's talents work together in sync toward a goal.

We've seen this happen with a women's softball team, for instance. When the coaches decided to set aside some time at the team retreat to identify and affirm the Signature Themes of each player, there was an amazing response. Not only did the coaches feel they knew their players better and could motivate them more effectively; the players also felt they knew their coaches better and trusted them more. The players felt they were more of a team once they understood they ways in which they each most naturally thought, felt, and behaved. This team cohesion can be a major contributor to a winning season.

Collaborating with Your Partner. Collaboration also operates in personal relationships with the significant people in your life. Over and over people have told us that learning about their talents changed their marriage, their relationship with their child, or their friendships. This change occurred as they saw the potential advantage of having complementary talents.

For example, Tamara and Will had been married for a while and seemed to have the same basic conflict on a continuing basis: Tamara would get enthusiastic about all the things they could do together, ways of redecorating the house, places they could travel on their next vacation, ways of investing their money, new ideas for raising the kids — the list went on and on. Will would critique each one, pointing out why it wouldn't work. This response deflated Tamara; she felt as if he was criticizing her and squelching her enthusiasm. Will, on the other hand, said all of her ideas just made him tired and most of them were beyond what they could afford to do.

But once they learned about each other's Signature Themes, Will recognized that Tamara's seemingly far-fetched dreams of all the things they could do were evidence of Ideation talents. They were simply her naturally powerful way of thinking through things — a brainstorming approach that would eventually lead her to something that would be great. Tamara then recognized that what she saw as criticism from Will was actually his Strategic talents at work: finding the best path in the quickest amount of time. When they understood this about each other, they realized what a great team they made — Tamara's ideas combined with Will's strategies meant that together they came up with the best ideas that could be implemented. They saw each other differently — and that changed their marriage for the better.

4. Control.

It may sound strange to include the word "control" in our list of ways of cleaning your glasses so that your relationships thrive. But if you remember our earlier comments about the way our brains tend to notice the negative more than the positive, you'll see why we've included a section on control in this chapter.

Control the "Shadow Side." We want to highlight two aspects of control. The first is the self-discipline to control the "shadow side" of the talents in your Signature Themes. To contribute at a refined level, all talents likely require complementary knowledge and skills, and your most powerful talents are not exempt. When you use your Signature Themes as an excuse for not treating others appropriately or for not doing a job that is expected of you, a rather obvious "shadow" is the result.

Here's an example: Someone whose greatest talents are in the Self-Assurance theme likely has a wonderful internal confidence that does not need to be fueled by the approval of others. As a result, this person is highly resilient, bouncing back from failures and difficult situations more easily than most. But what if this person with such wonderful internal confidence lacks sensitivity to other people's opinions or feelings, or stubbornly resists being "told what to do"? The "shadow side" of Self-Assurance talents could be an insensitivity to others or a resistance to being given instructions. When particularly powerful Self-Assurance talents are not managed through partnership with talents from other themes — such as Empathy or Adaptability — the confidence is there, but the insensitivity or resistance to others can harm or even eliminate its effectiveness.

Powerful talents from every theme have a shadow side that can be revealed when they operate in isolation. Command becomes bossiness; Significance turns into egotism; Maximizer manifests as relentless perfectionism; Belief becomes a judgmental attitude; Futuristic becomes the inability to enjoy the present moment. But never forget that when talents from these themes are productively partnered with those from other themes, little shadow is seen, and the potential for strength is greatly heightened. So Command rises to the occasion when courage is needed to right a wrong, and wisely does it without abusing others. Significance performs in a way that makes a real difference in the world, while Maximizer focuses on others' talents and coaches them to strength. Belief is rock-solid about what is most meaningful in life and actively lives through those beliefs, and Futuristic paints pictures that inspire "today" people to build the future.

Control the Conflict. The second aspect of control that we want to highlight is the ability to limit the damage that conflict can cause in our relationships by proactively resolving conflicts before they escalate. Conflict is inevitable in any relationship and simply means that there appear to be incompatible goals. But as any person with powerful Harmony talents will tell you, what appear to be incompatible goals can often be turned into win-win solutions.

Sometimes simple recognition of one another's uniquely powerful natures will make this happen. A person whose greatest talents are in Deliberative, for instance, may bump up against someone with dynamic Activator talents. The Activator is always ready to jump right in and may not understand the Deliberative person's need to carefully think things through. The talented activator may become impatient with what he or she sees as unnecessary delay, and the deliberative person may become frustrated at feeling rushed or pressured to take perceived "shortcuts." Conflict could easily result.

But when these people understand one another's greatest talents, the activator is able to see that the deliberative process results in excellent decisions and very few regrets, and it is valuable in making important decisions. And the more naturally deliberative person can learn to trust the activator's valuable sense of what needs to happen right away. By focusing on what each brings to the table and by finding common ground — both want to make a good decision and create a good outcome — the conflict can be managed proactively and productively.

Win-Win Strategies. This win-win strategy is one of several ways to manage conflict. Because conflict escalation creates some of the most damaging effects on people's relationships and physical as well as mental health, finding ways of averting or resolving conflict is important. In essence, escalating a conflict means returning fire with fire: Someone criticizes you or blames you for something and you reciprocate with nasty zingers of your own. This is a "no win" situation. Conflict and hostility have a dampening effect on your immune system, which means you're not protected against those cold and flu viruses that run rampant on college campuses. The bottom line: Unless you find ways of managing conflict in your life, you'll find yourself sick in bed much more often than you'd like.

When it looks like there is a potential conflict, keeping the focus on the problem rather than on the person is a first step to managing the confrontation effectively. Rather than blame the person, simply describe the situation and how you feel about it. The appropriate use of "I messages" can defuse a conflict. An "I message" emphasizes that you are taking responsibility for your own feelings about the situation. The basic recipe for an "I message" is this: "I feel (describe the feeling) when (describe the situation)." For example: "I feel hurt when you don't include me in your plans."

Many areas of potential conflict can be resolved by using "I messages." They become even more powerful conflict management tools when they are combined with an understanding of where the other person is coming from. Add to the equation an understanding of how the other person's unique combination of talents is shaping the way they see the world and how they communicate with you, and you have a recipe that can resolve most conflicts before they escalate.

For example, suppose you and your significant other have agreed to get together for dinner. Your greatest talents lie in Connectedness and Individualization; your significant other's most natural ways of thinking, feeling, and behaving come from the Consistency and Focus themes. Just as you are leaving work to get to the restaurant on time, one of your friends stops you in the parking lot to catch you up on the latest trauma in her life. With your Connectedness talents, you see the significance of each person who crosses your path. This interruption has happened for a reason — you are sure of it. Your Individualization talents lead you to focus in on what she is feeling and to become absorbed in her story — and to lose track of the time. Meanwhile, your significant other is waiting at the restaurant, exactly on time and hungrily concentrating on the menu — and how late you are. When you finally show up, the potential for a conflict is high.

But suppose you refine your Connectedness and Individualization talents by recognizing the importance of being on time and keeping your promises to your significant other. How would you have handled the situation differently, given that you still will see your friend's crossing your path as providential and will have a natural inclination to become absorbed in her story?

The situation has two possible endings. In one ending, there is conflict: The person who was kept waiting explodes, "You never think about anyone but yourself. I'm starving while you make time for everyone but me." The conflict escalates when you say, "There are more important things in life than your stomach. At least I have friends who need me."

But the ending could be entirely different if the waiting Consistency/Focus-talented person uses an "I message" such as, "Wow — I was worried something had happened to you when you were so late. I wish you had called to let me know what was going on. Were you delayed by someone who needed to talk to you?" And rather than escalate the conflict, the Connectedness/Individualization-talented person could say, "You're right about a friend who needed me — I felt it was important to make time for her. But it wasn't fair for you to be kept waiting — I should've called you and let you know what happened."

Whenever you feel a need to confront someone, think about it as an act of caring. Confrontation should not be a hit-and-run sport. Any confrontation should be conducted in the interest of maintaining and developing the relationship. Confrontation might hurt, but it should never be an attack on a person. Instead, the "attack" should be focused on the problem between you. This approach allows for win-win solutions and provides a positive future for the relationship. And as Archbishop Desmond Tutu said about his beloved South Africa as it tried to recover from decades of racial apartheid, "Without forgiveness, there is no future." You have to be willing to forgive a person who has wronged you, and to move on to a better place in the relationship.

5. Commit to cultivate.

The final action to take to clean your strengths-colored glasses and help your relationships thrive over the long haul is to commit to cultivate the relationship. Relationships are living, growing organisms. They require active nurturing to thrive, and they can die from neglect. The word *commit* implies intentional and lasting action. A commitment to cultivate a relationship means that you see the other person as worth an investment of your time and effort. That person matters to you.

People who show this level of commitment make great friends and lifetime partners. They know that affirmation of another person is what builds healthy relationships. They understand how important it is to express appreciation for the other person. But they recognize that no single other person can meet all their needs, so they cultivate many relationships. They have numerous "vital friends," as author Tom Rath calls them in his book of that name — different types of friends that meet different needs but are each necessary for feeling fully alive.

And even though 95% of people these days get married at least once, the research shows that a good friend can be just as good for your emotional and physical well-being as a good partner. The best predictor of positive relationships is emotional intimacy, not physical intimacy. Emotional intimacy involves disclosure of your feelings and what matters to you, being responsive to another person's needs, and feeling understood and cared for — all aspects of the best friendships as well as the best marriages and lifelong partnerships.

The "Real" You

And now it comes back to you. For any relationship to flourish, the people in it need to relate to one another authentically. When you clean your glasses so that you can see the talents and strengths in others, you also become a better version of yourself. In the words of the Velveteen Rabbit, you become "Real." If you remember that story from your childhood, you'll remember that the old Skin Horse tells the Velveteen Rabbit what it takes to become Real:

. . . when someone loves you for a long, long time, not just to play with, but *really* loves you, then you become Real. . . . It doesn't happen all at once. . . .You become. It takes a long time. That's why it doesn't often happen to people who break easily, or have sharp edges, or who have to be carefully kept. Generally, by the time you are Real, most of your hair has been loved off, and your eyes drop out and you get loose in the joints and very shabby. But these things don't matter at all, because once you are Real you can't be ugly, except to people who don't understand.

Chapter V

INSIGHTS INTO STRENGTHS
DEVELOPMENT

So far you have identified your areas of greatest talent in your Signature Themes and you have affirmed those with the significant people in your life. We've explored together the difference that strengths development can make in your relationships. Now it's time for the next step: strengths development itself.

A strength is the ability to consistently provide near-perfect performance in a specific task. You've learned that to build a strength, you first identify your dominant talents, then complement them with knowledge and skill.

Your ability to achieve excellence and get the most out of your life is connected to the extent to which you develop strengths. It all starts with talent, but it finishes with strength. That is, your Clifton StrengthsFinder assessment has helped you discover the themes in which your greatest talents probably lie, based on how you responded to the statements. But you have talents in all the themes — talents that can combine with your dominant talents in your Signature Themes. Combining talents, refining them with skills and knowledge, and then applying them to achieve excellence is what it means to build a strength.

To this point, we have focused on helping you identify, affirm, and celebrate your greatest talents. Now, it's time to focus on using them as the foundation of strengths development.

Principles and Strategies for Using Your Talents as the Foundation of Strength

Talents are like muscles. If you use them, they will help you achieve. Further, as you refine them, they will become even more capable of helping you achieve. Essentially, what you are able to achieve depends on the preparation and hard work you invest in building on your greatest talents by using them as the foundation for strengths.

Here are seven principles that you can use to make the most of your talents as you seek to develop strengths. Specific suggestions follow each principle.

1. Know your talents.

Of course, before you can begin to develop strengths, you must have somehow identified your greatest talents. By taking StrengthsFinder and affirming the talents in your Signature Themes, you have taken steps toward doing exactly that. As you continue reading and reflecting, you will refine that self-knowledge and solidify a foundation for strengths development.

Here is a simple exercise that can help clarify your talents. Take a piece of paper and write down each of your five Signature Themes. Next, write down at least one of your most powerful talents within each of those themes. Finally, write down an example of a time when you used each of those talents. If you can complete this exercise, you are building your awareness — and solidifying a foundation for strength.

2.   You must value your talents and assume personal responsibility for using them in strengths development.

If you do this, you will invest the time, energy, and other necessary resources. If you don't value your talents, you won't make the investments that their development requires. At first you may not see the value of your talents. To correct this misperception, please think of the two or three most important things you have ever done. Or ponder your proudest moment, the time when you were at your best, doing what you do best.

Next, identify a theme of talent that was at work in that situation. Then imagine having very little talent in that theme. What would have happened?

Now, from this perspective, do you value your talents enough to assume personal responsibility for making the most of them through strengths development?

3.   Talents are most powerful when inspired by a personal mission.

The philosopher Friedrich Nietzsche was quoted as saying, "He who has a 'why' to live for can bear almost any 'how.'"

What is the big "why" of your life? What are you ultimately trying to get done? What mission, purpose, or ultimate objective do you want to accomplish during your life?

These are the questions of "mission." A personal mission is the all-important task that you want to complete during your life. Your mission reflects what you hope will happen as a result of your actions. It is what brings meaning to your life.

Once you have formulated and clarified your personal mission, think about how your talents can help you fulfill it. Connecting your talents to your mission is critical because your mission motivates you to build on your talents by creating strengths, and your strengths will empower you to fulfill your mission. Also, new ideas about how you can develop strengths while fulfilling your mission might emerge. Make sure you write down these ideas and follow through on them.

4. Healthy, caring relationships facilitate the development of strengths.

Having at least one healthy, caring relationship while developing strengths is enormously helpful. Here are some characteristics of the empowering relationships in which talents seem to best flourish.

- There is mutual respect between you and the other person.
- You sense that he or she cares about you as a complete person.
- You can be open and honest with this person.
- You feel encouraged by being around this person.
- This person actively seeks to understand you.
- This person is a good listener.

In a healthy relationship that encourages strengths development, certain events likely will occur.

- You will talk about your talents and where you see them already working in your life.
- You will express the specific talents you want to build on and how you plan to go about doing it.
- You will report on your efforts and experiences as you try to develop strengths.
- You will receive feedback based on your reported efforts and experiences as you try to develop strengths.
- You will work together to form expectations about your talents, the tasks to which you want to apply your talents, and how you will develop strength in those tasks.

In essence, you will be trying to form a relationship with someone who inspires you to greatness.

5. Reliving your successes helps you develop strengths.

Every time you have performed with excellence, you have employed some of your greatest talents. Consider those successes for a moment. Can you recognize specific talents that played roles in your successes? If you can, you are claiming ownership of those talents, and you are building confidence in them — and in the process, you are building on those talents in strengths development.

To consider the roles your talents have played in your successes, try either talking or writing about them. As you try to capture in words the interplay between your talents and your successes, some powerful insights can occur.

6. Practice your talents.

As you use your talents over and over again, they will become refined. You will gain experience, and through that experience you will gain the knowledge and skills that will combine with your talents to create strength. Practice, practice, practice.

7. Teaching leads to learning.

To gain further understanding of talents, teach others about them. When you teach what you are learning, you are forced to learn it well enough to explain it to another person and answer his or her questions.

Now that you have gained a few insights into developing strengths, here's a challenge for you: Identify one specific task that you would like to perform at a level of excellence. Next, identify a theme in which you have talents that you believe can contribute the most to excellence in this task.

Finally, set a goal of refining that talent by using it at least twice as often as you are using it now.

Consider starting with one of your most dominant talents, possibly from your top Signature Theme. Beginning with the theme that brings you the greatest fulfillment would be a good idea, too.

For the rest of this chapter, we would like you to consider another set of strategies that offer insights and action ideas for developing strengths. Please locate and examine the strategies that are customized to your Signature Themes. As you examine them, try to select those that best fit the talents within your Signature Themes.

For each theme, we've identified several ways of refining those talents. Some of the strategies we list involve partnering with people who possess exceptional talents in other themes or managing the "shadow side" of the talent in order to create strengths.

USING YOUR TALENTS AS
THE FOUNDATION OF STRENGTHS

Using Your Achiever Talents as the Foundation of Strengths

Your Achiever talents hold potential for strength, which is the key to excellence. These statements provide interesting insights and tips that can help you use your talents as the foundation of strengths.

☐ You do not require much external motivation. Take advantage of your self-motivation by setting challenging goals. Set a higher goal every time you finish an assignment. Each goal met leads to the next goal set.

☐ Select challenging courses in which you have the leeway to work as hard as you want and in which you are encouraged to measure your own progress. You will feel challenged and alive in these environments.

☐ Own the fact that you might work longer hours than most people and that you might not need as much sleep as many other people do. Find the hours of the day when you are most productive and use that time for your most challenging work. Choose to study with other hard workers. Being in that kind of environment will energize you and bring out your best.

☐ You can become frustrated when others don't work as hard as you do. Your expectations for yourself and others are so high that you might be perceived as demanding. Consider taking on a complementary partner who has powerful Learner or Individualization talents that can help you gain insight into the unique motivations and capabilities of others.

☐ Even though you are full of energy, make sure you don't take on too many things at once. Pacing yourself can lead to even greater productivity and help you avoid burning out.

Using Your Activator Talents as the Foundation of Strengths

Your Activator talents hold potential for strength, which is the key to excellence. These statements provide interesting insights and tips that can help you use your talents as the foundation of strengths.

☐ Your commitment to doing something can be the "push" that many groups need in order to move from discussion to action. See it as your role in the group to ask for action items before the group dismisses.

☐ When insights or revelations occur, record them so you can act on them at the proper time. Writing them down enables you to act at the moment when speaking up may not always be appropriate.

☐ You are good at energizing others, once they understand the need for change. Partner with people who have exceptional Communication or Woo talents to tell a compelling story that will convince others of the need to act.

☐ When you feel the itch to take action, pause for a moment to ask yourself *why* you want action. If you can articulate that to others, they are more likely to get behind you.

☐ While you like to start things, follow-through is sometimes more difficult. Consider partnering with someone who has powerful Focus or Strategic talents, as that person will help you devise a plan to reach your goals.

☐ Sometimes you might get impatient with others who don't see the same need for action. Ask someone with powerful Developer talents to help you see the progress that is being made whenever you feel as though nothing is happening.

☐ Because it's so easy to send an e-mail when you are emotionally charged up about the need for action, ask a good friend to edit your e-mail before you press the Send button.

Using Your Adaptability Talents as the Foundation of Strengths

Your Adaptability talents hold potential for strength, which is the key to excellence. These statements provide interesting insights and tips that can help you use your talents as the foundation of strengths.

☐ Your ability to take things in stride means that you can be a calm and reassuring influence to people who don't handle change well. Use your exceptional ability to deal with stress by making yourself available to those who need your perspective.

☐ You enjoy the journey as much as you enjoy the destination. Help others find enjoyment along the way by encouraging them to see what's happening in the moment. You will enjoy the journey even more when there are others to share it with you.

☐ Sharpen your Adaptability talents by listening to your body. Just as you learn when to shift gears in a car as the RPMs get higher, you can learn to "shift gears" in your academic and work life by paying attention to when the pressure is mounting. By doing this, you can stay healthy and achieve even more.

☐ Your spontaneity can help others realize how many valuable experiences might be missed if they don't seize the moment.

☐ Because you live in the moment, you might find yourself easily distracted by new things that come along. You might be particularly likely to drop everything when your friends want you to go out with them. Connect your Adaptability talents with some of the talents in your other Signature Themes to help you remember the importance of what you're doing, so you'll be more likely to stay on task when necessary.

☐ Your natural ability to "go with the flow" enables you to make adjustments easily, but partnering with someone who has powerful Discipline, Consistency, or Arranger talents may give you added perspective on how to organize your schedule or be more efficient when the pressure hits.

☐ To others, things seem to just "fall into place" for you. Help them recognize that it isn't luck. You have a talent for adjusting to changing circumstances.

Using Your Analytical Talents as the Foundation of Strengths

Your Analytical talents hold potential for strength, which is the key to excellence. These statements provide interesting insights and tips that can help you use your talents as the foundation of strengths.

☐ You are at your best when you have well-researched sources of information and data to support your logic. Take the time to identify credible sources you can rely on. Determine the most helpful books, Web sites, or other sources that can serve as references.

☐ Take academic courses that will capitalize on your Analytical talents. Experimental psychology, chemistry, comparative religion, political science, statistics — all these areas can add knowledge and skills to your repertoire.

☐ Sharpen your Analytical talents by spending time talking to professors who research an area that interests you. Ask them to recommend books with which you can further explore their research.

☐ You naturally tend to dissect ideas and examine them carefully. While this process is almost instantaneous for you, it can be helpful to others if you explain what you are doing along the way. This explanation will help them buy into your conclusions at the end.

☐ You naturally simplify and connect related concepts. Look for people who are particularly talented in the Communication, Relator, or Positivity themes. They can help you clearly articulate what you see so naturally.

☐ Your natural skepticism and need to see the evidence can lead you into lively debates that are part of your process of becoming convinced. However, other people don't always enjoy debating issues as much as you do. Partner with people exceptionally talented in Relator, Empathy, or Communication, for instance, so that others understand you are critiquing ideas and not the people who have the ideas.

☐ Sometimes you may experience "analysis paralysis" — a continual need to gather more evidence and keep weighing the pros and cons before making a decision. Partner with Activator or Achiever talents to know when it's time to stop analyzing.

Using Your Arranger Talents as the Foundation of Strengths

Your Arranger talents hold potential for strength, which is the key to excellence. These statements provide interesting insights and tips that can help you use your talents as the foundation of strengths.

☐ You are happiest when you are part of a good team. You can offer your natural sense of organization and arrangement to keep a group project moving toward its goal.

☐ Complex, dynamic environments in which there are few routines are likely to bring out your best. Having daily opportunities to orchestrate solutions will keep you motivated and hone your Arranger talents even more

☐ Even the best systems routines can be improved. Refine your talent by challenging yourself to find ways to make these arrangements more efficient.

☐ Study successful systems and arrangements to understand the configurations that work best. Make notes and apply the patterns you see to your own systems.

☐ Discover the greatest talents of your friends, family, and coworkers. Help them figure out how they can match their talents to the tasks at hand.

☐ Organize a big event, or coordinate a homecoming celebration or club project. The challenge of a large-scale effort can energize you by highly engaging your Arranger talents.

☐ Your ability to multitask and prioritize allows you to manage several projects at the same time. Sometimes others may think you aren't listening to them if you continue to multitask while they are talking to you, so partner with Empathy or Individualization talents to recognize the nonverbal cues from others that tell you it's important to listen exclusively to them.

Using Your Belief Talents as the Foundation of Strengths

Your Belief talents hold potential for strength, which is the key to excellence. These statements provide interesting insights and tips that can help you use your talents as the foundation of strengths.

☐ Your energy comes from your sense of mission and purpose. Remember to connect the choices you make to the "why" so you will be fully committed.

☐ Think about the values you cherish most. Continue to clarify them so you can communicate them better to others

☐ To give voice to your values, partner with people who have exceptional talents in Communication or Woo. This approach will help others know who you are and how to relate to you.

☐ Actively seek roles that fit your values. In particular, think about joining organizations that define their purposes by the contribution they make to society.

☐ Listen closely to hear others' values and beliefs. Tune in to those as ways of connecting with other people.

☐ Consider defining your beliefs in more positive terms, focusing on what you are "for" rather than what you are "against." This might help you be perceived in a more positive way.

☐ Express your values outside of academics. Look to community service or volunteer work for opportunities that are a good fit with your value system.

Using Your Command Talents as the Foundation of Strengths

Your Command talents hold potential for strength, which is the key to excellence. These statements provide interesting insights and tips that can help you use your talents as the foundation of strengths.

- ☐ You naturally take charge. Learn to anticipate the situations in which others will look to you for leadership. Your comfort in "calling the shots" during a crisis can make a world of difference when time is of the essence.

- ☐ You don't shy away from confrontation. Taking time to listen to all sides can turn your ability to confront into real persuasiveness.

- ☐ In your relationships, seize opportunities to speak plainly and directly about sensitive subjects. You tend to put into words the issues that others are struggling with. When combined with empathy or listening skills, this can lead to a deepening of your relationships.

- ☐ Find a cause you believe in, and support it. You might be at your best when defending a cause in the face of resistance.

- ☐ Partner with people who have exceptional talents in themes such as Ideation and Strategic. They can help you see the big picture, and thus be even more persuasive.

- ☐ You can be a powerful advocate on behalf of others who are hesitant to express their concerns or who are powerless in their environments. Speak up for those who can't.

- ☐ You have no problem expressing your opinions freely. To avoid being seen as bossy, take the time to explain your position and its benefits.

Using Your Communication Talents as the Foundation of Strengths

Your Communication talents hold potential for strength, which is the key to excellence. These statements provide interesting insights and tips that can help you use your talents as the foundation of strengths.

☐ Capturing people's attention is one of the things you do best. Collect your stories so you'll have them handy, and practice so you'll get better each time you tell them.

☐ When you are presenting, listen closely to your audience. Watch their reactions to each part of your presentation. You will see that some parts prove especially engaging. After the presentation, take time to identify the parts that best caught the audience's attention. Draft your next presentation around these highlights.

☐ Collect your favorite stories, quotes, and poems to incorporate into your class presentations or papers.

☐ Gravitate toward learning environments that are characterized by dialogue and conversation. You will learn most and best when you get to talk as well as listen.

☐ Use your Communication talents to help others put their ideas or feelings into words.

☐ Keep a journal so you can clarify your thoughts and feelings by putting them in writing.

☐ Silence can sometimes seem uncomfortable to you. Partner with a person who has exceptional Empathy talents. He or she can help you gain a better sense of when others prefer quiet.

☐ Partnering with people who have powerful Positivity or Harmony talents can help develop your sensitivity to others' views.

Using Your Competition Talents as the Foundation of Strengths

Your Competition talents hold potential for strength, which is the key to excellence. These statements provide interesting insights and tips that can help you use your talents as the foundation of strengths.

- ☐ Winning motivates you. Strive to learn what it takes to win consistently. Adding that knowledge to your natural talents and your "game plan" will help you achieve even more.

- ☐ You like to keep score, so find ways of measuring your progress in every class. Ask your professors for feedback, so you know how you're doing.

- ☐ Seek competitive friends, especially those who will challenge you in some areas, so you can hone your talents even more.

- ☐ Comparing yourself to others motivates you to reach your full potential. If you are without peers, hone that talent by competing against yourself. Top your last performance. Make your next paper better than the last, your grades higher than before.

- ☐ Your opponents don't have to be other people. "Beating" poverty or injustice can be just as rewarding to you.

- ☐ Finding "win-win" solutions can lead to positive relationships with others while maintaining your own motivation.

- ☐ Choose your contests wisely. Learn to read a situation so you'll know when your likelihood of success is greatest.

Using Your Connectedness Talents as the Foundation of Strengths

Your Connectedness talents hold potential for strength, which is the key to excellence. These statements provide interesting insights and tips that can help you use your talents as the foundation of strengths.

☐ Because you can see connections that others may not see, your role in a group may be to help other people see connections and purpose in everyday occurrences.

☐ Your ability to see the web of relationships can lead to powerful learning experiences. Seek out classes where your open-mindedness and intuitive perceptions will be an asset.

☐ Schedule time for meditation and contemplation. Reflect on how your religious beliefs affirm your sense of connection to others, how your sense of connection gives you stability through your faith in people, and the role of "coincidences" in your life.

☐ Keep a journal so you can look back and see the experiences that support your sense of connection.

☐ Not everyone sees the connections you do or sees the role of faith that you may see. Rather than being disappointed by this, partner with someone with powerful Communication talents who can "tell the story" that you see so naturally.

☐ When others are in conflict or don't understand people who are different, your ability to see what people have in common can unite a group.

☐ Help those around you cope with unpredictable and unexplainable events. In particular, you can help people find meaning in even sickness and death. Your perspective will bring comfort.

Using Your Consistency Talents as the Foundation of Strengths

Your Consistency talents hold potential for strength, which is the key to excellence. These statements provide interesting insights and tips that can help you use your talents as the foundation of strengths.

☐ Your role in a group can be to level the playing field. For instance, you can be a leader in your community by providing disadvantaged people with the platform they need to show their true potential.

☐ Take the time to think through the "rules" that are closest to your heart. These rules might be based on certain values or "nonnegotiables" in your life. The greater your own clarity about these rules, the more comfortable you will be with individuality within these boundaries.

☐ Cultivate a reputation for recognizing those who really deserve credit. Ensure that respect is always given to those who truly performed the work. You can be the conscience of your group.

☐ You probably become frustrated when you see inequity. Partner with people whose Adaptability or Positivity talents can help you keep things in perspective when this happens.

☐ You are good at setting clear expectations, but not everyone has the same passion about some of your rules. They may see you as picky. Explaining why these expectations are important to you can help others relate to you better.

☐ If you live on campus, you may have an opportunity to help write fair policies in your residence hall. You instinctively know what is fair and equitable for all; when you practice putting into words what equitable treatment is, your Consistency talents will be honed even more.

☐ Your sense of consistency can make you an excellent role model. In community service settings or volunteer work, focus on teaching these valuable principles to those around you in order to build trust.

Using Your Context Talents as the Foundation of Strengths

Your Context talents hold potential for strength, which is the key to excellence. These statements provide interesting insights and tips that can help you use your talents as the foundation of strengths.

- ☐ If you are part of a team or club, help it strengthen its culture by understanding its roots. For example, collect symbols and stories that represent the best of the past and its heroes.

- ☐ Read historical novels, nonfiction books, or biographies. You will discover many insights that will help you understand the present. You will think more clearly when you see these historical examples.

- ☐ Before starting your papers or projects, ask your professors for examples of excellent papers so you can see how others have successfully approached the assignment.

- ☐ When you are contributing to a group project, start by learning about the past experiences of each member.

- ☐ Because you value the lessons of the past so much, you may have a tendency to feel it's important to do things the way they have been done in the past. Partner with people who have powerful Strategic talents to see the best way to approach challenges or new opportunities.

- ☐ Think about your past successes. What can you learn from them that can help you in the tasks you presently face?

- ☐ Partner with people who have exceptional Futuristic talents. They can help you build an even greater bridge from the past to the future.

Using Your Deliberative Talents as the Foundation of Strengths

Your Deliberative talents hold potential for strength, which is the key to excellence. These statements provide interesting insights and tips that can help you use your talents as the foundation of strengths.

☐ You are naturally adept at preventing problems by seeing the risks ahead of time. Communicate to others what you are seeing so they will trust your good judgment.

☐ Because you are careful and thoughtful, taking time to think before you speak, others may not feel they get enough feedback from you. Let people know when they can expect input or a decision from you.

☐ Partner with someone who has exceptional Self-Assurance talents. That person can give you the confidence to stick with the good decisions you've made.

☐ Your thoughtful approach gives you the foresight you need to make wise decisions. Be sure to set aside some time each day for yourself. You have a need for your own space, so negotiate with your roommate or partner about having some time and space to yourself when you need it.

☐ Offer your Deliberative talents to people who would like help thinking through their decisions. You will soon be sought as a valuable sounding board.

☐ Your talents are most needed when the decision is important or has lasting consequences. Practice "letting go" of the less important decisions so you can apply your talents fully when it matters most.

☐ Don't let anyone push you into revealing too much about yourself too soon. Check people out carefully before sharing confidential information. You naturally build friendships slowly, but your small circle of good friends can be a treasured resource.

Using Your Developer Talents as the Foundation of Strengths

Your Developer talents hold potential for strength, which is the key to excellence. These statements provide interesting insights and tips that can help you use your talents as the foundation of strengths.

☐ Your role in any setting usually involves facilitating growth. Roles in teaching, coaching, or managing might prove especially satisfying for you, so seek out those opportunities now through service learning or campus organizations.

☐ Keep a scrapbook or digital photo album of the people you have helped learn and grow. Look at it often, and remind yourself of the positive effect you have had on the world.

☐ Notice when your friends learn and grow, and enhance their growth by sharing your specific observations.

☐ You are a natural encourager. Take the time to call or e-mail people who need your encouragement most.

☐ Create an action plan for success and list the intermediate steps you can take to reach your goal. Identify strengths you can build to ensure your success.

☐ You probably will flourish when you help less fortunate people or disadvantaged kids see that their talents are opportunities for development.

☐ Recognize that while you notice the "baby steps" of progress, others may expect bigger steps. Be able to articulate these intermediate steps to others.

Using Your Discipline Talents as the Foundation of Strengths

Your Discipline talents hold potential for strength, which is the key to excellence. These statements provide interesting insights and tips that can help you use your talents as the foundation of strengths.

☐ Your role in any setting is often to provide structure and keep things organized.

☐ Research new organizational or time-management systems. They can make you even more efficient and confident.

☐ Create routines that make you follow through systematically. Share your reasons for those routines with other people.

☐ Try to maintain a structured lifestyle. Find a place for everything. Keeping your personal space neat is something you do naturally, but don't neglect it when you get stressed. It will serve to stabilize you when the pressure hits.

☐ Time for planning is a key to your achievements. Honor this aspect of who you are rather than trying to "wing it" as some of your friends may encourage you to do.

☐ Develop a calendar, and make things fit into it. Identify when and where to study and work. Have a time each day to go over your schedule for the next day.

☐ Others may confuse your Discipline talents with rigidity. Be ready to explain to others how your structure and organization enable you to pack more effectiveness into your day.

Using Your Empathy Talents as the Foundation of Strengths

Your Empathy talents hold potential for strength, which is the key to excellence. These statements provide interesting insights and tips that can help you use your talents as the foundation of strengths.

☐ You have a natural ability for getting in touch with the feelings of others. Hone this talent by refining the words you use to name the feelings you experience and those you observe in others. Help others name their feelings, as well. People who can name their feelings seem to work better with other people.

☐ At times your Empathy talents can drain you, if you are not careful to develop rituals at the end of each day that allow you to "decompress."

☐ Absorbing others' emotions sometimes leads to experiencing those emotions yourself. Establish clear boundaries between yourself and those to whom you connect.

☐ If you pick up negative emotions more easily than the positive, you may need to intentionally become more aware of positive emotions. This proactivity can keep you more balanced and emotionally rewarded.

☐ You are an emotional person, and you need to express your own emotions to someone you trust.

☐ Sometimes it is important to be silent. You likely have the talent to let people understand you know how they are feeling, without even talking. Refine your nonverbal communication skills.

☐ Let others know you can feel their pain and that tears are okay. Communicating that you understand their feelings builds trust.

Using Your Focus Talents as the Foundation of Strengths

Your Focus talents hold potential for strength, which is the key to excellence. These statements provide interesting insights and tips that can help you use your talents as the foundation of strengths.

- ☐ Some of your greatest contribution as a team member might come as you help others set goals. When you work on group projects, take responsibility for summarizing what was decided, defining when these decisions will be acted upon, and setting a date when the group will reconvene.

- ☐ Take the time to write down your goals and post them where you can refer to them often. You will feel more grounded and in control of your life when you keep your eye on the target.

- ☐ Your powerful goal orientation could at times supersede your people orientation. Make sure the people you care about understand that you appreciate an opportunity for intense focus, but also that you are always happy to hear them knock on your door.

- ☐ Partner with Ideation or Strategic talents before honing in on a goal, so you can gain confidence that your Focus talents are aimed in the most effective direction.

- ☐ When given assignments, clarify timelines and expectations in advance. You become discontent with what you see as "busy work."

- ☐ You can spend long periods of time concentrating on one thing. This allows you to be highly productive, but can lead to even greater excellence if you set aside those periods of time intentionally and let others know why you're doing that.

Using Your Futuristic Talents as the Foundation of Strengths

Your Futuristic talents hold potential for strength, which is the key to excellence. These statements provide interesting insights and tips that can help you use your talents as the foundation of strengths.

- ☐ Your natural anticipation of a preferred future enables you to overlook the pain and problems of today. Help others anticipate and imagine their futures as well.

- ☐ Take time to think about the future. The more time you spend considering your ideas about the future, the more vivid your ideas will become. The more vivid your ideas, the more persuasive you will be.

- ☐ Work on the words you use to describe the future. Partner with Communication, Ideation, or Woo talents to use vivid visual images and storytelling to become even more persuasive about what the future holds.

- ☐ Help others think about the future. You can be a guide or coach who inspires others to dream.

- ☐ Because you can see what's coming, you can be better prepared for it. Partner with Discipline or Arranger talents to be organized in your preparation for the future.

- ☐ Your natural ability to anticipate the future may mean you are not "in the present" to the extent you could be. Spend time with your friends who have powerful Adaptability, Context, or Positivity talents to fully enjoy the moment.

- ☐ Check out futurist Web sites and read futurist books and magazines. They will fuel and refine your vision for the future.

Using Your Harmony Talents as the Foundation of Strengths

Your Harmony talents hold potential for strength, which is the key to excellence. These statements provide interesting insights and tips that can help you use your talents as the foundation of strengths.

☐ Your greatest offerings to any group are your willingness to compromise and your tolerance for differing views. You can help others in your group reach agreement more quickly because of your significant talents in seeing areas of common ground.

☐ When working with others, stress the value of reaching consensus.

☐ Build a network of people with differing perspectives. Rely on these people when you need expertise. Your openness to these differing perspectives will help you learn.

☐ When two people are arguing, ask others in the group to share their thoughts. By increasing the number of voices in the conversation, you are more likely to find areas where all parties can agree. You can draw people together.

☐ You know that win-win solutions are the best for everyone and move a group forward with greater confidence. Hone your Harmony talents by working with more diverse groups each time.

☐ Recognize that there may be times when conflict is inevitable and even necessary. In such situations, partner with those who have powerful Command or Activator talents to promote more positive group interactions during the conflict.

☐ Sometimes your deep desire to "keep the peace" leads you to stay silent when you disagree with someone. Recognize that sharing your feelings can lead to a win-win solution for yourself as well as others.

Using Your Ideation Talents as the Foundation of Strengths

Your Ideation talents hold potential for strength, which is the key to excellence. These statements provide interesting insights and tips that can help you use your talents as the foundation of strengths.

☐ Your role in a group may be to brainstorm new and creative possibilities. With your abundance of ideas, this approach can be more exciting and more productive for your group.

☐ If you get bored quickly, think about how you can expand your world — your social network, your academic opportunities, and your community involvement.

☐ You have a natural capacity to consider issues from multiple perspectives. Because you see what others cannot, it's important for you to make it clear when you brainstorm that you are laying out a diversity of perspectives to consider, rather than that you are committed to a certain one.

☐ You have a high rate of creative productivity in your life. Partner with Strategic or Futuristic talents to help you hone these ideas into even higher levels of creativity.

☐ Keep an "idea journal." When an idea comes to you, write it down and list the actions you can take to make it happen. This constructive step can energize you.

☐ Because ideas come to you so easily, you might not recognize how valuable they could be to others. Work to communicate your ideas effectively to inspire others.

☐ Partner with Intellection, Maximizer, Analytical, Discipline, or Achiever talents to harness all your ideas and turn the best ones into reality.

Using Your Includer Talents as the Foundation of Strengths

Your Includer talents hold potential for strength, which is the key to excellence. These statements provide interesting insights and tips that can help you use your talents as the foundation of strengths.

☐ Choose roles in which you are continuously working and interacting with people. You will enjoy the challenge of making everyone feel involved.

☐ Look for opportunities to bring together people of diverse cultures and backgrounds. You can be a leader in this area.

☐ Help those who are new to a group get to know other people. You will be adept at quickly making people feel accepted and involved. Bring outsiders in by recognizing their talents and asking them to contribute to the group through those talents.

☐ You are naturally aware of the pain others feel when they are left out. Hone this talent by adding the skills it takes to physically include "outsiders." Sit next to the loner, or talk to the person others are ignoring.

☐ Inclusion also can involve information. Think about who should know about upcoming activities or opportunities. Who should be involved in key decisions? Be the one who includes others in information sharing.

☐ Draw out others' opinions in a group setting. Speak up for the importance of including everyone's feelings.

☐ There is a time to include; there also may be a time to not include. By increasing involvement, you increase diversity and input — but you also increase complexity. There may be times when being somewhat selective with your Includer talents could create the same good result but with greater efficiency.

Using Your Individualization Talents as the Foundation of Strengths

Your Individualization talents hold potential for strength, which is the key to excellence. These statements provide interesting insights and tips that can help you use your talents as the foundation of strengths.

☐ You instinctively understand how very different people might be able to work together effectively. Use this talent to help create partnerships, teams, and groups that complement each other.

☐ Become an expert in describing your own talents and style. For example, answer questions such as these: What is the best praise you ever received? How often do you like to check in with your professors? What is your best method for building relationships? How do you learn best?

☐ Your understanding of what is right in people could play a key role in helping others recognized and reach their potential. Help your family and friends plan their futures by helping them define their uniqueness.

☐ You know that one size does not fit all. Make your family and friends aware of each other's unique needs. Soon people will look to you to explain the motivations and actions of others.

☐ Study successful people to discover the uniqueness that made them successful.

☐ You are at your best when you are surrounded by people who appreciate you and encourage you to become more of who you are. Actively seek one-to-one relationships. This will give you the greatest opportunity to use and develop your Individualization talents.

☐ Because you easily see each person as unique and you are able to appreciate their individual value, your praise for others may be misperceived as indiscriminate and therefore insincere. Specifically noting what you find praiseworthy in an individual and highlighting that quality can help others gain a greater appreciation for them as well.

Using Your Input Talents as the Foundation of Strengths

Your Input talents hold potential for strength, which is the key to excellence. These statements provide interesting insights and tips that can help you use your talents as the foundation of strengths.

☐ You may be a natural researcher. Hone this talent by acquiring knowledge of specific research methods. Consider taking a research methods course in psychology or sociology.

☐ Identify possible areas of specialization and actively seek more information about them. Seek out faculty in those areas and pick their brains outside of class.

☐ You are naturally curious but may need to intentionally schedule time to feed your mind. Take time to read books and articles that stimulate you, or to travel to new places. Your Input talents need regular "feeding."

☐ Partner with Focus or Discipline talents to channel your Input productively and to organize all you've discovered so that it is more readily available for you to use.

☐ Devise a system for storing and easily locating the information you gather. This system can be as simple as a file for all the articles you have clipped or as sophisticated as a computer database.

☐ Identify situations in which you can share the information you have collected with other people. Being able to share your "stuff" with others will make for a better learning experience for everyone.

☐ A sense of when to stop seeking information is just as valuable a talent as your thirst for information. Set a time limit on your Internet searches so you'll be able to get your papers done. Mark the best sites so you can return to them when you have more time.

Using Your Intellection Talents as the Foundation of Strengths

Your Intellection talents hold potential for strength, which is the key to excellence. These statements provide interesting insights and tips that can help you use your talents as the foundation of strengths.

☐ You typically ask great questions. As a result, people may seek you out for your ability to serve as a valuable sounding board.

☐ Consider beginning or continuing your studies in philosophy, literature, or psychology. You will enjoy subjects that stimulate your thinking.

☐ Although you are a natural thinker, make a point to schedule time for thinking. Use this time to muse, reflect, and reenergize. You need quiet time to refuel.

☐ Keep a journal and take time to write regularly. These ideas will serve as grist for your mental mill, and they might yield valuable insights. Writing might be the best way to crystallize and integrate your thoughts.

☐ Find people who like to talk about the same issues you do. Make time to hang out and talk about these issues.

☐ Sometimes your energetic debate of a philosophical issue can be intimidating to those with lesser talents in this theme. Partner with Empathy or Positivity talents to recognize when others are beginning to feel uncomfortable.

☐ Practice putting your thoughts into plain language so others can better understand your thinking. Remember that others cannot read your mind. Give them a glimpse at what's happening inside your head, and translate it into language they can relate to.

Using Your Learner Talents as the Foundation of Strengths

Your Learner talents hold potential for strength, which is the key to excellence. These statements provide interesting insights and tips that can help you use your talents as the foundation of strengths.

- ☐ You are energized by the challenge of keeping up with constantly changing fields. Take courses in a wide variety of subjects in order to keep your interest levels high.

- ☐ Identify your own learning style. How do you learn best — through doing? By reading? When you listen to experts? When you are able to work with friends in a group? Find your best learning environments and organize your life so that you are in these environments more. Use your Learner talents to learn about yourself — and achieve more in the process.

- ☐ Find ways to track the progress of your learning. If there are distinct levels or stages of learning within a body of knowledge or skill, celebrate your progression from one level to the next. If no such levels exist, create them for yourself. (For example, set a goal of reading five books on the subject.)

- ☐ You love the challenge of a steep learning curve, so beware of learning plateaus. Seek opportunities to stretch yourself with more difficult or complex assignments and courses.

- ☐ Spend time talking to your professors. Soaking up their knowledge and learning from them will be enjoyable and highly motivating.

- ☐ Learning is meaningful to you. Keep the mentality that you are never done learning, not even when school is over. You are a lifelong learner. Keep a journal of "lessons learned" that you can go back to often.

- ☐ You love the process of learning so much that the outcome may not matter to you. As a result, you may have a number of unfinished projects that you plan to come back to "someday." Partner with Strategic, Activator, Focus, or Achiever to make your Learner talents even more productive and purposeful.

Using Your Maximizer Talents as the Foundation of Strengths

Your Maximizer talents hold potential for strength, which is the key to excellence. These statements provide interesting insights and tips that can help you use your talents as the foundation of strengths.

☐ You have a nose for excellence. This talent means you are able to give helpful input and advice about who does what well. In group assignments, your role may be to help the group capitalize on each person's talents most effectively.

☐ Seek opportunities to help other people succeed. Consider coaching your intramural team or volunteer to be a Big Brother or Big Sister. Your focus on talents will prove particularly beneficial. For example, because most people find it difficult to describe what they do best, start by arming them with vivid descriptions.

☐ To maximize most effectively, focus on your greatest talents, as they are your best opportunities for strengths. Acquire and refine related skills. Gain relevant knowledge. Keep working toward strength in your areas of greatest potential.

☐ Develop a plan to use your talents outside of academics. Consider how they relate to your mission in life and how they might benefit your family or the community.

☐ Study success. Spend time with people whose talents you admire. The more you understand how talents lead to success, the more likely you will be to create success in your own life.

☐ Be careful that your discriminating sense about excellent performance doesn't extend to discrimination about people. Find the best within each person you encounter and let them know what you see.

☐ Not everyone likes to hear how they can improve. Make the most of your Maximizer talents by giving people encouraging feedback before suggesting ways they could be even better.

Using Your Positivity Talents as the Foundation of Strengths

Your Positivity talents hold potential for strength, which is the key to excellence. These statements provide interesting insights and tips that can help you use your talents as the foundation of strengths.

- ☐ Your best contribution is often to highlight the positive. In your friendships or in class, you can help others see the "silver lining" in the cloud.

- ☐ You tend to be more enthusiastic and energetic than most people. When others become discouraged or are reluctant to take risks, your attitude will provide the motivation to keep them moving. Over time, others will start to look to you for this lift.

- ☐ Help others see the things that are going well for them. You can keep their eyes on the positive, which will be encouraging to them as well as being rewarding for you.

- ☐ Because people will rely on you to help them rise above their daily frustrations, arm yourself with good stories, jokes, and sayings. Never underestimate the effect that your wonderful sense of humor can have on people.

- ☐ You know how to throw a party. Find opportunities to celebrate the significant people and events in your life. Partner with Developer talents to celebrate even the small achievements.

- ☐ You bring energy and fun to group projects. Let others know that your optimism is not naivete or a denial of reality. Help them understand it's a natural, valid, and productive focus on what is right and good.

Using Your Relator Talents as the Foundation of Strengths

Your Relator talents hold potential for strength, which is the key to excellence. These statements provide interesting insights and tips that can help you use your talents as the foundation of strengths.

☐ You tend to be at your best when you are part of a stable group of friends you can trust. Join a regular study group in your challenging classes so you can stay motivated to achieve.

☐ If you are new on campus, get to know the people who live near you. Early relationships with them can benefit you in the long haul.

☐ You don't want to be close friends with everyone. You're probably most comfortable around people who accept you for who you are. As you get to know people, listen for their talents and imagine how their ways of naturally thinking, feeling, and behaving could complement your own.

☐ Learn as much as you can about the people with whom you want to relate. Your interest will be a catalyst for trusting relationships.

☐ No matter how busy you are, take time for your friends. They are your fuel.

☐ You're probably more comfortable in informal environments. Smaller classes, and even smaller colleges, are likely to be the kind of environments where your talents will flourish.

☐ You need time to get to know people before trusting them, but trusting only your close group could mean you miss out on the valuable input of those not in your group.

Using Your Responsibility Talents as the Foundation of Strengths

Your Responsibility talents hold potential for strength, which is the key to excellence. These statements provide interesting insights and tips that can help you use your talents as the foundation of strengths.

☐ You may work best when given the opportunity to follow through on your commitments as you see fit. When you work on class projects, tell the group members that you don't need to check in during a project, just at the end. You can be trusted to get it done.

☐ Working with others who also have powerful Responsibility talents is satisfying to you. Clarify your roles in advance and decide who will take ownership of what tasks, so that you don't step on each other's toes.

☐ You have an instinctive sense of how to do things right. To best understand you and your talents, others might need you to explain your choices and how you know what's right.

☐ People with exceptional Responsibility talents like to know they have met others' expectations. Tell your professors that their feedback about the quality of your work is important to you.

☐ You naturally take ownership of everything you are involved in. Be sure to share some of that responsibility with others so they can grow and develop as well.

☐ Ask your professors for the objectives of an assignment, then figure out how to fully meet them — or even go above and beyond expectations.

☐ Learn to manage your Responsibility talents by deciding what you will stop doing if you take on a new responsibility. With your high level of psychological ownership, you may take on more than you can handle unless you are able to keep the mental image of a balanced scale in your mind.

Using Your Restorative Talents as the Foundation of Strengths

Your Restorative talents hold potential for strength, which is the key to excellence. These statements provide interesting insights and tips that can help you use your talents as the foundation of strengths.

☐ Solving problems is par for the course for you. Because you can identify root issues and directly address needs, you may work exceptionally well with challenging or demanding people.

☐ You may be adept at finding the flaws, but you are also adept at finding solutions. Be sure to partner your solution talents with your problem-spotting talents for maximum effectiveness.

☐ You can usually put your finger on what is wrong in relationships. Your friends may come to you for advice or help with their problems.

☐ Learn to complement your Restorative talents by partnering with people who have powerful Positivity talents. Their natural optimism will keep your problem-solving from becoming pessimism.

☐ In community service or volunteer work, your best role may be as a troubleshooter for the organization.

☐ Sometimes the best way to fix a problem is to empower others to fix it themselves. Rather than rush in with a solution, partner with Developer talents to coach others in solving their problems themselves. You will refine your talents as you help others learn and grow.

☐ You may be your own toughest critic. You label it "honesty." Develop your talent for truth-telling about yourself to include the honest truth about your valuable talents.

Using Your Self-Assurance Talents as the Foundation of Strengths

Your Self-Assurance talents hold potential for strength, which is the key to excellence. These statements provide interesting insights and tips that can help you use your talents as the foundation of strengths.

☐ You may feel best in roles in which you are charged with persuading people to see your point of view. Your Self-Assurance, especially when combined with powerful Command or Activator talents, can be extremely persuasive.

☐ You are comfortable expressing a difference of opinion when you are not personally convinced of the value of an idea or approach. Build on your Self-Assurance talents by becoming well informed on issues so you can speak for those who may be hesitant.

☐ Appeal to your internal compass to determine appropriate actions. Trust your instincts on both large and small issues. Hone those instincts by noticing the physical cues when your "gut feeling" is right.

☐ You don't have a great need for direction or support from others. This could make you particularly effective in situations that require independence in thinking and action.

☐ Recognize and actively contribute the value of your Self-Assurance talents in situations where confidence and initiative are crucial.

☐ Your Self-Assurance may be misperceived as arrogance or self-importance, so making the most of your talents in this theme may mean partnering with Connectedness or Empathy talents to tune in to cues from others on how you are being perceived.

☐ Partner with people whose Input or Intellection talents can complement yours as you gather information on class selection, choosing a major, or deciding on an approach to a project. Your inner compass will become even more fine-tuned.

Using Your Significance Talents as the Foundation of Strengths

Your Significance talents hold potential for strength, which is the key to excellence. These statements provide interesting insights and tips that can help you use your talents as the foundation of strengths.

☐ You probably are most engaged and effective when you have some sense of control and choice. Seek independent projects that give you freedom to excel.

☐ Your reputation is important to you, so decide what you want it to be, and tend to it in the smallest detail. Identify and earn a designation that will add to your credibility, write an article for the campus newspaper that will give you visibility, or volunteer to speak in front of a group that will appreciate your achievements.

☐ Identify your best moment of recognition or praise. What was it for? Who gave it to you? Who was the audience? What do you have to do to recreate that moment?

☐ Being seen as credible, professional, and successful is important to you. Consider joining student organizations tied to your major. These can be opportunities to develop your credentials and professional expertise as you head into a career or to graduate school.

☐ You value appreciation and affirmation. Tell the significant people in your life how important their feedback and support are to you. Their words can motivate you to even higher levels of achievement.

☐ Be aware that you often want the significant people in your life to be proud of you. You enjoy the challenge of meeting others' expectations. Share your dreams and goals with your family or closest friends. Their resulting expectations of you will keep you reaching for those dreams and goals.

☐ Above all, you want to make your mark on the world. You deeply care about making a difference. Decide which actions are likely to have the most impact in an area you care about. Take risks and step into the spotlight.

Using Your Strategic Talents as the Foundation of Strengths

Your Strategic talents hold potential for strength, which is the key to excellence. These statements provide interesting insights and tips that can help you use your talents as the foundation of strengths.

☐ Your best contribution to a group may be to discover the path to success. Because you can do this so quickly, it may look as though you are "winging it," but explaining yourself along the way will help others understand what you see.

☐ Make full use of your Strategic talents by scheduling time to carefully think about a goal you want to achieve and the paths you might take to reach it. Remember that time to contemplate is essential to strategic thinking.

☐ You naturally see alternatives more readily than others. Offer your Strategic talents when others are "stuck." Your insights can allow them to go over, under, or around, rather than through.

☐ Partner with people who have powerful Ideation or Strategic talents to talk about the alternative directions you see. Detailed conversations like this can help you become even better at anticipating.

☐ Sometimes others misinterpret your Strategic talents as criticism or naysaying. Realize that you can develop your Strategic talents by taking into consideration what is already working well and what others have already done.

☐ You are capable of quickly seeing the need for Plan B where others cannot. You may need to slow down and explain your strategy to others so they can appreciate the wisdom of your solution.

☐ You may have great talent in seeing possibilities that are invisible to others. To motivate others, communicate your vision and the steps that will make it reality.

Using Your Woo Talents as the Foundation of Strengths

Your Woo talents hold potential for strength, which is the key to excellence. These statements provide interesting insights and tips that can help you use your talents as the foundation of strengths.

☐ You may be naturally adept in social settings. As you "work the room," you come alive. Spend time every day interacting with a great number of people — it likely energizes you.

☐ Consider being a peer leader for new-student orientation. You are especially good at helping new people feel comfortable.

☐ Partner with Strategic, Learner, or Achiever talents to harness your "woo power" in academic tasks. A strategic use of Woo talents, for instance, can target your powerful energy toward the wisest use of your time and resources.

☐ Learn the names of as many people as you can. In class, call your classmates by name to help them learn each other's names and to build a sense of community.

☐ Consider running for student government office. You are a natural campaigner. Understand, however, that you might enjoy the campaigning more than holding the office.

☐ Your ability to get people to like you is very valuable. Use that talent to make positive changes in your world. In social situations, take responsibility for helping put more reserved people at ease.

☐ Practice specific ways to engage others. For example, research professors before you meet them so you can find some common ground.

Chapter VI

CONSIDERING STRENGTHS WHEN PLANNING YOUR EDUCATION

Personal excellence should always be at the forefront of your mind when you're planning an education. Accordingly, each and every step in the planning process should lead to higher and higher levels of personal achievement.

The essence of planning every aspect of an education that will lead to personal excellence, right down to each course you select, lies in answering one question:

Will it help you become all that you have the talent and opportunity to be?

To help you answer this question in planning your education, we will share the lessons we have learned about excellence from studying great learners, educators, and leaders.

Five Truths That Great Learners, Educators, and Leaders Know About Excellence

1. Our talents hold the key to excellence.

Many people mistakenly think that their greatest potential for growth is in their weakness. But this is not true. We grow and develop most when we are working on and working with our most natural talents.

2. Simply having talents isn't enough to produce excellence. Talents must be built upon in strengths development, and the resulting strengths must be applied. This requires practice and hard work.

Some people think that merely possessing talents ensures easy achievement of excellence. But great learners, educators, and leaders know that this is pure myth. As in any area of life, achieving excellence in education requires meticulous, painstaking preparation and hard work.

3. Excellence requires that you have a clear idea about what excellence is, what it looks like, and what is required to reach it.

For example, as a student, you should know what an excellent paper or essay reads like in order to write one. The image of excellence must be crystal clear.

One "straight A" college student developed a unique way of forming such a mental image of excellence that helped him write papers. First, he reasoned that if an article or a book gets published, at least one person must think it's excellent. But he further reasoned that different people might have varying ideas about excellence. So, this young man went to the library and found book reviews on each of the books he was assigned in his classes.

By reading book reviews on the books in his classes, he was able to form a mental image of what was, and what was not, excellent about a particular book. This also gave him ideas about how to critically analyze the materials presented in his classes. Armed with this information and the mental images that had emerged, this young man was prepared to write papers and essay examinations on the texts assigned in his courses.

4. Focusing on one area of talent at a time is the best route to excellence.

There is a danger in diffusing your attention and effort by focusing on too many things at once. Taking one area of talent at a time and developing it to the maximum moves you to excellence most efficiently. Once a person has reached excellence in one area, a framework for and an understanding of excellence in other areas is likely to emerge. Your own questioning mind sets a direction and can fuel your pursuit of excellence. Your curiosities reveal where you want to grow, develop, and learn more.

5. It is also important to realize that many talents — all working together and strategically applied — are necessary to produce excellence.

Achieving excellence isn't easy. Most strengths are rooted in not just one talent, but two, three, or even more. This is one of the reasons why reaching levels of excellence takes considerable time and practice.

Think about the meaning of your talents in combination. Begin by focusing on your two most powerful Signature Themes. How do your talents within these themes interact with one another? What does that interaction tend to produce? Now, consider your talents in your third Signature Theme. How do your talents in these three themes interact and influence one another?

Consider what you want to get out of college. In essence, what are your desired outcomes? Ponder the ways in which you want to develop as a person.

Think about the skills you'd like to develop. For example, do you want to hone your writing, mathematical, and/or problem-solving skills? Perhaps you are most interested in developing your thinking skills. Consider the knowledge you want to gain. In what areas do you want to be more knowledgeable than you are today? What information, insights, and understandings will you need for the future?

Now, think about the matter of awareness. Perhaps you would like to learn more about your own culture and the meanings of various traditions. Maybe you'd like to gain more knowledge of various modes of artistic expression or understand the nature of science.

Consider career outcomes. Do you hope that college will help you identify a career, or prepare for it? If so, what do you need to learn while in college to be effective in your career?

On an entirely different level, you might look at the college experience as a time to clarify or affirm your values. Maybe you see college as a time to set a direction for your life and make a group of commitments regarding yourself and your future.

Whatever the case, the first focus of planning a college education should be on your desired outcomes. Clearly, those outcomes are directly related to the decisions you make not only before you begin college, but also while you're in college. Each term, you will make a group of decisions regarding what classes you will sign up for and who your professors will be. We urge you to make informed choices about classes and professors, as they will have a direct impact on your outcomes.

Last, but not least, consider graduation requirements, the structure of the degree, and requirements you may need to fulfill to enter a particular career or graduate-school program.

Questions to Help Your Educational Planning

Academic advisors are marvelous college resources. Staff and advising faculty offer a great deal to your educational planning process.

To help you prepare for meeting with your advisor and to help you make wise involvement decisions, we have listed several questions for your thoughtful reflections.

1. **Self-Assessment of Talents**

   - Which of your Signature Themes describe you best?

   - Which of your Signature Themes hold the talents you use most frequently?

   - In which of your Signature Themes are your talents most highly refined?

   - Which talents do you want to maximize the most in college?

2. **Motivations, Dreams, and Desires About College**

   - What are you hoping will happen while you are in college?

   - What do you want to be able to do as a result of going to college?

   - Imagine that you have graduated from college and you feel great. What would make you feel so great about your experience?

   - Which of your talents do you believe will be most instrumental in helping you fulfill your dreams and desires for college?

   - Which of your talents will you be planning to develop through classes and extracurricular activities?

   - What images come to your mind when you think about fully maximizing your talents through strengths development?

3. **Self-Assessments of Intellectual Interest and Curiosities**

   - What do you seem to learn with the greatest ease?

   - What have your teachers complimented you about?

   - What do you have a burning desire to know and understand?

4. **Vocational, Career, and Graduate School Aspirations**

   - To date, what experiences have been your most fulfilling?

   - Which careers seem most interesting and attractive to you?

   - In what career would you be able to best use your greatest talents?

   - Given your general career interests and vocation, what types of graduate-school training will you need?

- Which courses and college opportunities can help you best prepare for your vocation, career, and graduate school?

5. **Time and Energy Demands**

- What are your family responsibilities, and how much time will they require each week?

- How many hours per week must you work to meet your financial responsibilities?

- To achieve highly in each of your classes, how much time will be required each week?

- Which of your most natural talents can you count on to make your efforts time- and energy-efficient?

6. **Self-Assessment of Academic Abilities**

- In what areas do you have the greatest academic abilities?

- On what types of tests do you score highest?

- What has been your favorite type of assignment?

- What subjects do you most enjoy studying ?

- How have your greatest talents helped you succeed in the past?

- What academic tasks employ your most powerful talents?

- In which academic tasks would you like to discover how to better apply your greatest talents?

7. **Degree Structure and Requirements**

- What courses must you take to graduate?

- Where do you have flexibility in fulfilling your graduation requirements?

- What are the graduate-school entrance requirements for the programs you are considering?

- What classes will best prepare you to enter the career or graduate schools you are considering?

Final Considerations in Planning Your Education

Your answers to the previous questions will help you create a plan to achieve your desired educational outcomes — but there certainly is more to consider.

Equally important is the issue of timing. When should you take certain college classes? When should you become involved in the various college programs, services, activities, and resources that are available?

In answering each of these questions, and in making your plan for education a reality, you should make strengths development "priority one." Doing so will help you gain confidence, build your motivation, heighten your sense of direction, and lead you to an enjoyable experience in taking on the many challenges and opportunities offered by the college experience.

Chapter VII

DEVELOPING ACADEMIC
STRENGTHS IN COLLEGE

You have considered the importance of talents in planning your education to achieve personal strengths. Now, it is time to plot out how to build on your talents to develop leadership and other strengths directly related to your college experience.

Four key factors capture the basic aspects you should consider when planning an education that will lead to personal excellence.

Four Key Factors That Will Determine Your Achievements in Academics, Career, and Beyond

1. Your beliefs about your talents to achieve

Never underestimate the power of what you believe — it will directly affect your achievements. What you believe about your talents can affect *whether you will even attempt to achieve.* Your beliefs directly influence your emotions, attitudes, behavior patterns, and motivation.

2. How well you know, understand, and value your talents

One of our primary goals is to increase your understanding of and appreciation for your greatest talents. This forms the basis for increasing your confidence and for building achievement patterns.

3. The extent to which you apply your talents through strengths

You should provide the initiative for designing your education around your talents. This is likely to produce superior results, because you won't be "getting" an education, you'll be creating one. And it will be based on who you really are and the person you have the capacity to become.

4. Your motivations, desires, and goal-setting practices

Numerous studies identify motivation as the single most important factor in academic achievement and graduation from college. Specifically, they point to two important motivational dynamics: First, you must have multiple motives for achieving and persisting. Second, these motives must be important to you personally. Having only one reason for achieving (for example, to make more money or to please someone else) usually results in lesser achievement.

Four Tips for Developing Academic Strengths in College

Your overall academic experience can be greatly enhanced by the perspective and direction you take in setting goals and making key decisions. Consider these four suggestions.

1.   Define college success in terms of maximizing your talents through strengths development.

If you are going to assume responsibility for your college experience, you must come to grips with defining success for yourself.

So, what is the best outcome of college that you can imagine? Most people would say getting a 4.0 GPA, graduating Magna Cum Laude, getting a well-paying job, or gaining admission to medical school, law school, or some other graduate or professional school. These are good, but your considerations should go well beyond your college years. Defining college success in terms of identifying and building upon your greatest talents emphasizes *building yourself into a person of excellence.*

2.   Select classes on the basis of your talents and strengths.

Considering your talents is particularly important as you select classes for the early portion of your college education. In these first couple of years, it is especially important to build your confidence by following your talents. Far too many students who enroll in college never graduate, and many of those who drop out do so in the first year. Why? Quite frequently, the reason is that they have selected classes that don't suit their talents. As a result, they don't experience the success they expected, and then they become frustrated and disillusioned and eventually give up.

Be sure to continue to apply the strengths approach during the rest of your college career. This means that *every time* you select your classes, ask yourself two questions: (1) Which of my talents will I be able to apply in this class? and (2) What strengths will this class help me create? If you don't know the answer to either of these questions, get more information about the classes you are considering. If you have to say "none" to both questions, you must ask yourself why you are enrolling in the class in the first place.

These comments may be controversial, so let's be clear: We are not anti-liberal arts, nor are we trying to undermine the need for all students to have certain basic skills. We are certainly not trying to limit students' exploration of new fields.

What we oppose is educational practices that give students placement tests to find out what students *can't do* or *don't know* — and then force them to focus first on where they struggle before they can learn about their most naturally powerful talents.

3.   Consider your talents when selecting extracurricular activities.

To gain maximum benefits from college, think about college as a total experience in which you *purposely become as deeply involved as possible.* This means making college the focal point of your life. Becoming personally involved might include forming study groups, meeting with professors, and making use of campus programs and services. If possible, live on campus or near campus — and with other students — or at least form close relationships with people from college.

As you make decisions about extracurricular involvement, seek opportunities to build on your talents in strengths development. For example, form relationships with professors and students who share your talents. Become involved in clubs and organizations that provide opportunities for you to use or develop strengths.

4.   Choose your college jobs by considering the opportunities they provide to develop strengths by following your talents.

Most college students must work in order to make ends meet. That is a reality, but it is also true that employment during college presents another opportunity to build on your talents. Therefore, carefully consider where you'll be employed and what type of work you'll do. The most ideal situation would be (1) to work on campus so you can increase your involvement, and (2) to work in a job where you can use and build on at least some of your most natural talents. That way, you will be doing more than just earning money.

Strategies for Applying Your Talents in Academics

To help you determine how you can best apply your greatest talents toward strengths in academics, we have collected feedback from thousands of top-achieving college students. Through interviews, focus groups, case studies, and surveys, we have gathered insights about how these successful students perceived and applied their most powerful talents in several areas of academics.

Now, it's time to take a look at strategies that can help you use talents in your Signature Themes for achievement in various aspects of your academic life. Once again, locate and examine the strategies that are customized to your Signature Themes. As you do this, you may want to consider the items that are already helping you achieve and those that may help you achieve at an even greater level of excellence.

APPLYING YOUR TALENTS
IN ACADEMICS

Applying Achiever Talents in Academics

These insights and action ideas can help you apply Achiever talents to achieve in various aspects of your academic life.

General Academic Life

- ☐ Set at least one clearly defined and measurable goal for each of your courses at the beginning of the term. Document your progress toward every objective in an academic-achievement journal.

- ☐ Identify the most important fact, philosophy, concept, or law you learn in each class each week. Notice recurring patterns. Pinpoint discoveries.

- ☐ Set one or two "stretch" targets, such as earning a specific grade-point average, winning honors status, or being named to the dean's list.

- ☐ Ask to review papers, projects, research studies, or tests of several students who consistently earn higher grades in a class than you do. Try to equal or surpass one or two things they do.

- ☐ Seek opportunities to apply several of the ideas and concepts you have learned. Address groups and conduct demonstrations so others can benefit from what you know.

- ☐ Ask each of your professors to clarify their expectations for your performance. Emphasize that you intend to exceed the minimum course requirements.

Study Techniques

- ☐ Review your goals-achievement log. Look for evidence that you are progressing toward your objectives. Outline the steps you took to acquire one particular skill or master one key concept.

- ☐ Pay close attention to your body clock. Decide when your mind is most alert. Use this insight to your advantage when scheduling time to study.

- ☐ Decide whether your productivity, efficiency, and ability to retain essential information increases when you study with a tutor, a classmate, a group, or alone.

☐ Observe classmates to discover who shares your commitment to hard work. Form a study group composed of individuals who invest time, effort, and energy in scholarly pursuits.

☐ Reach consensus as a study group about attendance, starting and ending times of meetings, strategies to eliminate distractions, and the sharing of class notes.

☐ List everything you must do to prepare for a test, complete a project, conduct research, or finish an assignment. Prioritize activities. Set a deadline for each one. Then methodically carry out your plan.

Relationships

☐ Intentionally nurture friendships with people who are as driven as you are.

☐ Talk to students taking advanced-level courses in your major field. Ask them to describe the choices they made in the past that contribute to their success today.

☐ Realize that your natural inclination to study for as long as it takes inspires other achievers. Learn the names of these individuals. Add them to your study buddy network.

☐ Seek opportunities to work with professors on research projects, laboratory experiments, and writing for publications.

Class Selection

☐ Choose challenging, effective classes taught by instructors who have reputations for helping students reach their educational goals.

☐ Sequence the order in which you take classes. Each term, enroll in one course that is more demanding than any you have ever taken. Repeat this process each semester.

☐ Recruit diligent, serious, and earnest students to register for the same demanding classes you are taking. Realize that you will challenge one another to excel.

☐ Sign up for classes that cover unfamiliar topics. Understand that you are motivated by challenges.

Extracurricular Activities

☐ Join clubs that have members who share your strong work ethic.

☐ Advance toward your academic and career goals by enrolling in rigorous classes, volunteering on campus, performing community service, working part time, and participating in intramural or extramural sports.

☐ Elect to join organizations where your accomplishments will be recognized. Choose groups with goals that align with your own. Insist on establishing deadlines for reaching each objective.

Applying Activator Talents in Academics

These insights and action ideas can help you apply Activator talents to achieve in various aspects of your academic life.

General Academic Life

☐ Initiate classroom discussions. Suggest topics. Take sides in debates. Help your fellow students learn faster and learn more.

☐ Find the answers to questions that you anticipate the instructor will ask on upcoming tests and quizzes.

☐ Instigate conversations with your peers outside the classroom. Center these on topics related to a recent lecture given by your instructor or a visiting professor.

☐ Take charge of small-group conversations, projects, presentations, and experiments. Distinguish yourself by transforming plans into tangible results.

☐ Waste no time finishing the first draft of a writing assignment. Immediately seek feedback from a teaching assistant or your professor. Incorporate some of their constructive suggestions in your second draft.

Study Techniques

- [ ] Lead study groups. Participate in the life of the mind. Urge members to share their best ideas. Give timid individuals permission to explore topics, raise questions, and work on projects.

- [ ] Jot down one or two key thoughts as you read an article, story, or the directions from a project. Use these insights to shape the group's discussions.

- [ ] Draw quiet individuals into conversations, debates, planning, and discussions. Call on them by name. Probe when they respond to questions with one- or two-word answers.

- [ ] Read ahead to prepare for class lectures. Compose two or three questions not offered in the textbook to ask your instructor. Intentionally change the classroom atmosphere from one of passive listening to active participation.

- [ ] Stay physically active to remain mentally engaged in your studies. Eat. Pace. Take breaks to stretch. Test your ideas with your study group. Press for their honest opinions.

Relationships

- [ ] Surround yourself with individuals who are restless to start working on projects and assignments. Associate with people who welcome and respond to your directives.

- [ ] Identify classmates who automatically know when the time for planning has expired and the time for action has arrived.

- [ ] Initiate conversations with professors outside the classroom. Make appointments with them to confirm expectations, clarify course requirements, and establish deadlines.

- [ ] Volunteer to chair group discussions, facilitate brainstorming sessions, or spearhead projects. Observe your classmates' relief at not having to be in charge.

Class Selection

☐ Choose a major field of study about which you are passionate. Realize your success hinges on your being fully engaged. Opt for courses that involve hands-on activities, lively verbal exchanges, and interesting experiments.

☐ Check the course syllabus for information about projects, field trips, extra reading, and independent study options. Avoid classes that restrict your pace and methods. Honor your need for speedy results and changes of pace.

☐ Attack your assignments immediately. Refuse to procrastinate. Turn in your work ahead of schedule. Enjoy the satisfaction of being done. Analyze how you avoid the pitfalls of "analysis paralysis" and excessive preparation.

☐ Persuade your professor to give you permission to invent your own assignments with the understanding that they must satisfy the course requirements and learning objectives.

Extracurricular Activities

☐ Join clubs and try out for athletic teams with jam-packed rosters of events. Avoid groups with a reputation for meeting a lot but accomplishing very little.

☐ Volunteer for activities such as constructing a Habitat for Humanity® house, serving as a Big Brother or Big Sister, acting in community theatre productions, conducting nature walks, running to raise funds for worthwhile causes, or coaching a youth team.

☐ Be the change agent for a stalled project. Study the original action plan. Determine why momentum was lost. Convince group members they can put the undertaking back on course. Recruit several energetic individuals to help implement the new initiative.

☐ Campaign for an office in campus government. Influence potential voters to cast their ballots for you.

Applying Adaptability Talents in Academics

These insights and action ideas can help you apply Adaptability talents to achieve in various aspects of your academic life.

General Academic Life

☐ Live in the moment. Calm yourself before an exam with positive self-talk. Recall your personal history of dealing with surprises on tests.

☐ Leverage your ability not to feel overwhelmed by multifaceted assignments. Document three to five instances during the day when you successfully juggled competing tasks.

☐ Understand that you can balance academic demands with social commitments, extracurricular activities, and part-time jobs. Describe how you managed to make progress on all fronts last week.

☐ Challenge yourself by taking courses that involve experiments. Compare your flexibility to that of various classmates. Notice how you make adjustments to produce desired outcomes.

Study Techniques

☐ Analyze your study habits. Do you plan and then improvise as circumstances change? Or do you improvise minute by minute rather than plan?

☐ Choose study partners who are serious yet share your easy-going, relaxed work style. Avoid individuals who are tense and anxious. Make a list of potential study buddies.

☐ Look for irony, humor, and the unexpected in your studies. Stimulate your own and others' thinking by discussing the relevance of each discovery.

☐ Make notes about how your study habits vary depending on the situation. Ask yourself these questions: Do I need the pressure of a test or deadline to force me to study? When am I most likely to ignore intriguing distractions? Least likely?

☐ Designate places to which you can retreat when you need to give your full attention to your studies. Choose venues where the potential for interruptions and extraneous noise is significantly reduced.

Relationships

☐ Surround yourself with individuals who, like you, pause to take in the world's loveliness as it appears. Identify people who automatically put aside what they are doing to watch a sunset, listen to rustling leaves, or enjoy the arts.

☐ Help classmates, coworkers, and friends overcome difficulties that stymie their progress. Capitalize on your ability to take things as they are rather than rail against life's surprises.

☐ Encourage some people to turn to you when plans must be modified or altogether scrapped. List the people who realize you are approachable and responsive.

☐ Invite one or two highly organized and time-conscious people to become your study buddies. Discuss ahead of time how they can help you be more efficient. Explain how you can infuse fun into their studies.

Class Selection

☐ Follow your interests when choosing classes. Keep your options for a major open until you have explored several disciplines. Partner with an advisor who can help you accelerate your decision-making process to avoid additional tuition costs.

☐ Register for more classes than you intend to take. After the first week of class, drop elective courses you find uninteresting.

☐ Transfer out of classes taught by instructors whose teaching style bores you. Transfer into the classes of professors who stimulate students' thinking.

☐ Take advantage of the drop-add period. Note the date by which you must complete this process without risking a failing grade or loss of money.

Extracurricular Activities

- ☐ Join organizations that sponsor events that demand flexibility in terms of planning as well as execution. Capitalize on your ability to monitor and adjust.

- ☐ Convince teammates of the importance of not fighting change. Outline the benefits of letting go of the original plan in order to try a new process.

- ☐ Recall two or three instances where you successfully redirected the emotional energy of people paralyzed by unexpected news or sudden changes in the group's plans.

- ☐ Consider participating in extemporaneous speech tournaments or improvisational theater. Play to your ability to capitalize on each moment.

Applying Analytical Talents in Academics

These insights and action ideas can help you apply Analytical talents to achieve in various aspects of your academic life.

General Academic Life

- ☐ Examine data, collect facts, and read material for discussions. Anticipate problems. Ask questions to discover others' perspectives on issues. Clarify your own position.

- ☐ Reduce situations, problems, opportunities, projects, assignments, and debates to their key components. Stay two to three steps ahead of everyone else's thinking by pinpointing cause-and-effect relationships.

- ☐ Deduce the consequences of someone's decisions, inaction, and pronouncements. Use logic to trace the effects of scientific breakthroughs, ethical lapses, and legal judgments.

- ☐ Prove to your classmates that there is an equal and opposite reaction to every action.

- ☐ Read assignments before class. Find information to support or discount the position taken by the author of the textbook.

☐ Reinforce your understanding of the subject matter by reorganizing and expanding your classroom notes. Insert subtopics and subpoints.

Study Techniques

☐ Notice the subtle nuances of a subject. Question the authors' conclusions. Flag topics for scrutiny. Refuse to accept blindly whatever appears on the printed page.

☐ Assess why you do quite well in one course but not as well in others. Evaluate your study habits, note taking, listening, capacity for asking questions, and reading comprehension.

☐ Draw "mind maps" to illustrate the placement of each element of a theory or aspect of a concept as well as a story plot. Investigate until you logically link facts or numerical data with results.

☐ Record questions as you read. Ask: "What is missing here?" "What questions should the author have answered?" "What biases are evident and not so evident?"

☐ Make sense of discussions. Write what you heard and said. Identify comments, conclusions, and arguments that lack supporting facts or data.

Relationships

☐ Break down situations. How is the same set of facts likely to be interpreted by someone older than you? Younger than you? From a different cultural, ethnic, religious, socio-economic, or racial background?

☐ Identify your biases before taking sides on an issue. Evaluate your own thinking before challenging others' biases.

☐ Incorporate into your study group individuals who thoughtfully assess the value of information, details, research findings, evidence, people's comments, and events.

☐ Refrain from saying what is on your mind until you have figured out everything. Realize that this reduces the tension between yourself and others.

Class Selection

☐ Select professors with reputations for presenting lessons in a logical, sequential manner. Avoid instructors who present a confusing jumble of unrelated ideas, facts, theories, illustrations, or philosophies.

☐ Select courses that will use your talent for critical thinking. Be open to the sciences and mathematics as well as literature, history, and the arts.

☐ Consider the soundness, validity, and reliability of information presented in your textbooks and by your professors.

☐ Dismiss erroneous statements, flawed theories, and illogical conclusions, as well as prejudiced opinions. Risk being the solitary voice of reason.

Extracurricular Activities

☐ Gravitate to organizations known for their commitment to the use of logic and reason.

☐ Volunteer to serve on campus committees charged with proposing recommendations to key decision-making bodies such as the student senate, the school board, and the state legislature.

☐ Join the debate team. Delve deeply into the chosen topic. Fully research both sides of the issue. Prepare logical arguments from both perspectives. Continue to build both cases to clearly define strong positions.

☐ Accompany an athletic coach to scouting and practice sessions for a week. Identify three to five ways you can combine your love for a particular sport with your analytical abilities. Consider plays the team could run, or the types of physical talents required for the various positions.

Applying Arranger Talents in Academics

These insights and action ideas can help you apply Arranger talents to achieve in various aspects of your academic life.

General Academic Life

- ☐ Note all assignments, tests, and appointments on a calendar. Use your planner to coordinate your personal and academic activities.

- ☐ Read all directions prior to taking tests. Allot appropriate time to each section of the examination.

- ☐ Be prepared to stop working on a current project and begin a new one in case the situation changes.

- ☐ Keep all notes related to a topic on one page. Make them easily accessible for studying, test taking, and research papers.

Study Techniques

- ☐ Prioritize your studies. Identify the most important tasks based on deadlines, percentage of final grade, and difficulty. Balance your workload.

- ☐ Underline, highlight, and take notes in margins of books. Summarize main ideas.

- ☐ Pick locations where you can study. Figure out why certain environments are better for particular subjects.

- ☐ Schedule study breaks to clear your mind. Check on other projects, or make phone calls.

- ☐ Break each study session into distinct modules. Plan time to read, write, work on projects, eat, sleep, exercise, and socialize.

Relationships

- ☐ Recognize that you can change your personal agenda to meet others' demands. Ponder how you adjust your living and working environment to help others reach their goals.

☐ Assemble people to work on major class projects and prepare for exams. Name the ways you help your study buddies distribute and redistribute learning tasks.

☐ Create opportunities for group members to teach each other.

☐ Plan activities to mark the end of projects and success on exams.

Class Selection

☐ Help your instructor plan class projects. Volunteer to assemble needed supplies. Distribute materials to students and collect them at the end of class.

☐ Figure out ways for your classmates to manage their workloads so that they complete projects on or before the due date.

☐ Suggest independent study options to your advisors and professors. Design your own curriculum.

☐ Examine the course catalogs from other schools in the vicinity. Substitute some of these courses for ones on your degree or certification plan.

Extracurricular Activities

☐ Orchestrate your study time so that extracurricular activities can fit into your schedule.

☐ Get involved and stay busy. Mix non-academic projects, appointments, meetings, and tasks into your day or week.

☐ Coordinate routine activities, special events, trips, parties, and projects for your teammates.

☐ Mix and match the talents, knowledge, skills, and experience of your classmates to launch a project, move toward a goal, or produce desired outcomes.

Applying Belief Talents in Academics

These insights and action ideas can help you apply Belief talents to achieve in various aspects of your academic life.

General Academic Life

☐ Write an academic mission statement for yourself. Integrate your core values, such as a leaving the world better than you found it, curing AIDS, ending violence, or affirming the dignity of each human being.

☐ Discover ways to weave your core values into routine classroom assignments. Write and speak about topics directly related to your beliefs.

☐ Read about individuals who stood up for their convictions in the face of resistance. Determine who inspired these people to dedicate their lives to great and noble causes.

☐ Debate an issue like: "Money is the true source of happiness." Argue for and against this proposition. Ask yourself, "How was my position strengthened when I could incorporate my beliefs into the argument? How was my position weakened when I had to defend the opposing point of view?"

Study Techniques

☐ List your top three to five beliefs on a piece of paper you can use as a bookmark. Filter whatever you are reading and hearing through the lenses of these core values.

☐ Assess whether you are allocating enough time to classes, projects, and assignments that add meaning to your life.

☐ Suggest alternative topics for reading and research to your professors. Match your preferred assignments to one or more of your core values.

☐ Form a study group of individuals with whom you share one or more important belief. Ask each member to describe how these core values contribute to his or her success as a student.

Relationships

☐ Tell your classmates and professors about the ideas, causes, and projects you are most passionate about.

☐ Encourage others to tell you when your intensity inspires them and when it overwhelms them. Maintain an ongoing dialogue to ensure that they understand you.

☐ State what you believe is right and wrong. Help others grasp what you value and why you value it.

☐ Notice instances when you willingly inconvenienced yourself to come to the aid of a specific person or group. Ask, "Which of my core values drove this behavior?"

Class Selection

☐ Enroll in ethics classes. Learn to evaluate the rightness of decisions in fields such as science, medicine, business, government, religion, and environmental protection.

☐ Risk advocating your beliefs in class discussions as well as conversations with classmates and instructors.

☐ Choose courses taught by professors known for their strong beliefs, even when their values clash with yours. Realize that considering the values of others can help you refine your own.

☐ Select classes that challenge you to clarify, reinforce, defend, and live out the guiding principles of your life.

Extracurricular Activities

☐ Figure out ways to spend quality time with your family. Make a point of going home or calling to show you are thinking of them on birthdays and special holidays.

☐ Consider running for a campus office. Build your campaign platform on values-oriented issues that matter greatly to you. Inform potential voters about what you stand for and why.

☐ Practice speaking a foreign language by helping a refugee family adapt to their new country and its customs.

☐ Serve meals at a local homeless shelter. Deliver Meals on Wheels®. Take time to visit with each shut-in.

Applying Command Talents in Academics

These insights and action ideas can help you apply Command talents to achieve in various aspects of your academic life.

General Academic Life

☐ Ask probing and pointed questions during discussions and lectures by professors. Realize that your questioning mind accelerates your learning.

☐ Take charge of your college education. Play the lead role in shaping your degree or certification plan. Refuse to leave these decisions to an advisor.

☐ Challenge facts presented in textbooks, the media, and class presentations. Critique your instructors and classmates. Search for the truth.

☐ When a particularly interesting class discussion is ended due to time constraints, express to your professor your wish that he or she would continue the discussion in an office visit.

Study Techniques

☐ Join study groups known for debating ideas, theories, and problems.

☐ Use your Command talents to clarify rather than intimidate. Understand that some clear-thinking individuals may become flustered under pressure.

☐ Give your instructors feedback about what you most enjoy and benefit from in their classes.

☐ Develop hypotheses and thesis statements that you must defend in writing or oral presentations. Recognize that you are more engaged when you must build a case to support your ideas.

- [ ] Play devil's advocate — that is, argue the opposing view — for fun and benefit when the opportunity arises. Warn people that you like to draw others into debates.

Relationships

- [ ] Assume the leadership role in groups, especially when you have knowledge, skills, expertise, and experience others lack.

- [ ] Notice which classmates rely on you to ask the professor questions. Provide this service for those who are intimidated by the instructor's knowledge or demeanor.

- [ ] Study your mannerisms, vocal tone, and content of your messages when talking with authority figures. Pinpoint how you present yourself as a person worthy of their time and undivided attention.

- [ ] Explore ways that you can serve others by giving orders and making demands. Identify individuals who are comfortable and content following your lead.

Class Selection

- [ ] Select classes that require you to plan your own curriculum. Acknowledge your desire to make your own academic decisions.

- [ ] Take classes in which you are expected to voice your opinions, argue, draw conclusions, take sides, and make recommendations.

- [ ] Choose classes taught by instructors who take a position and demand that students challenge it.

- [ ] Enroll in courses with professors who are secure enough to welcome your combative learning style.

Extracurricular Activities

- [ ] Gravitate to organizations in which you can envision yourself being a key decision maker.

- [ ] Realize that you threaten some people with your forceful style.

- [ ] Opt to participate in activities where you must persuade people to embrace your ideas, plans, solutions, or philosophies.

☐ Join groups in which you are expected to sell products and services, solicit donations, and raise money.

Applying Communication Talents in Academics

These insights and action ideas can help you apply Communication talents to achieve in various aspects of your academic life.

General Academic Life

☐ Participate in class discussions. Enhance your own and others' comprehension by talking through the key points.

☐ Respond to questions with thought-provoking answers.

☐ Illustrate scholarly concepts with real-life examples. Help others learn in the process.

☐ Capture your audience's interest by telling stories to amplify an idea, concept, theory, scientific law, philosophical point, ethical quandary, or historic event.

Study Techniques

☐ Converse about the subject matter until you fully understand it.

☐ Tell others about your solutions, theories, concepts, and ideas before presenting them in class. Acknowledge that this is how you refine your thinking.

☐ Notice how your classmates rely on you to engage the professor in dialogue. Realize that you are quite comfortable doing this.

☐ Entertain your study group with anecdotes that make history, mathematics, science, languages, or the arts come alive in their minds.

Relationships

☐ Take the pressure off quiet, timid individuals by doing most of the talking.

☐ Cheer up people with accounts of your own and others' humorous escapades.

☐ Plan at least four meetings each term with professors who are good listeners. Take advantage of the fact that they expect you to do most of the talking.

☐ Express your philosophical views, goals, pet peeves, and opinions so others can learn about you as a person.

Class Selection

☐ Take classes from professors who encourage students to interrupt lectures to share stories or offer examples that amplify a concept.

☐ Select classes in which you will be graded for participation in class discussions.

☐ Register for courses that require you to make presentations.

☐ Enroll in theatre arts, speech, and communications classes.

Extracurricular Activities

☐ Affiliate with a speakers' bureau in which the members address campus and community groups.

☐ Try out for the speech team. Concentrate on dramatic interpretation to hone your storytelling skills.

☐ Audition for plays even if you are not a theatre major.

☐ Campaign for elected office, or be a candidate's spokesperson.

Applying Competition Talents in Academics

These insights and action ideas can help you apply Competition talents to achieve in various aspects of your academic life.

General Academic Life

☐ Regard grades as your scorecard. Invest more effort in classes where the results of tests, papers, and projects are posted for all to see.

- ☐ Monitor your grade-point average by the week, month, or academic term. Compare your class ranking to that of your closest rivals. Realize that striving for the highest GPA leads you to excel.

- ☐ Clarify how professors weight class participation, final exams, presentations, laboratory experiments, and research projects. Continuously monitor your grades and class standing.

- ☐ Study your opponents — that is, your classmates. Identify each one's strengths. Evaluate their study strategies. Continually compare your results to theirs.

Study Techniques

- ☐ Seek out highly competitive people and study with them. Know that you will push each other to learn more, faster. Figure out how to manage the inevitable undercurrent of tension that will exist.

- ☐ Pit yourself against a fellow student to increase your chances of being the first person to finish the paper, test, or project.

- ☐ Establish measurable and meaningful academic goals. Use these to force yourself to reach the highest levels of productivity, mastery, or quality.

- ☐ Identify the best students in your classes or major area of study. Investigate what they routinely do to be number one.

- ☐ Quiz your professors about their criteria for earning the highest grades in their classes. Explain that you aim to understand the material better than anyone else in the class.

Relationships

- ☐ Intentionally surround yourself with competitive people.

- ☐ Aim to know something special about every person in the class by the end of the first month. Use these insights to your advantage when you vie against them.

- ☐ Help classmates understand that you are hardwired to have the last word in casual conversation, classroom discussion, or formal debate.

Class Selection

☐ Apply at universities and departments within universities where admission standards are highly competitive. Make sure that objective, meaningful, and measurable criteria are used to determine who is selected.

☐ Take advanced-level classes to enhance the odds of winning important academic scholarships, grants, internships, and fellowships.

☐ Select instructors who encourage rivalry between students.

Extracurricular Activities

☐ Try out for the debate or speech team. Audition for a play, first chair in a section of the orchestra, or a featured dancing role.

☐ Play competitive sports. Risk being a walk-on to win a spot on an athletic team.

☐ Check your department's bulletin boards for opportunities to enter contests. Gravitate to contests sponsored by student and professional organizations in your major area of study.

☐ Run for leadership positions such as student senate, class president, club officer, or sorority/fraternity chairs. Campaign to win.

Applying Connectedness Talents in Academics

These insights and action ideas can help you apply Connectedness talents to achieve in various aspects of your academic life.

General Academic Life

☐ Ask yourself, "What life lessons am I supposed to learn today through my studies and the challenges they present? What is at work here that is much more important than passing a test or getting a good grade?"

☐ Search for linkages between your coursework and what you're being called to contribute to the entire human family today and in the future.

☐ Examine how your life is inextricably tied to those of people in other parts of the world and from the past. Name as many of these connections as you possibly can.

☐ Find ways to build bridges of understanding between classmates as well as between students and their professors. Realize that you're motivated to show people how world events and close-to-home circumstances bind each individual to all humankind.

☐ Start each day by reading an inspirational verse or a piece of scripture from your faith. Sit in silence with these words for 10-15 minutes. Open yourself to surprising discoveries about how to best approach your studies and other people.

☐ Keep a journal. Let your ideas and feelings flow freely. Write without editing. Find purpose and meaning in your personal and academic life.

Study Techniques

☐ Pray for guidance before you begin studying. Ask that your mind be freed of worries and distractions. Implore yourself that you can truly trust that all will be well.

☐ Concentrate on your breathing before starting a test, making a presentation, or working on a project. Spiritually unite yourself with students around the world who are facing similar challenges at this very moment.

☐ Silence competing scholarly demands of your life by practicing daily meditation. Master the art of letting go. Embrace the art of living in the present moment.

☐ Be mindful of the abundance of good things. Realize that more than one student can earn a good grade or receive the professor's approval.

☐ Energize your body, heighten your awareness, and soothe your soul with inspiring background music. Create a calm environment in which to study, work on projects, solve problems, research, write, and prepare for exams.

Relationships

- ☐ Converse with individuals who realize that life is a complex web of interdependence among all human beings, living things, events, and inanimate objects.

- ☐ Share with curious observers how and why you can remain calm in the midst of uncertainty, losses, successes, defeats, progress, and setbacks.

- ☐ Help others understand that you view all life as a continuous, ever-widening circle without beginning or end. Explain how every thought, word, and deed impacts people far and near.

- ☐ Bring ideas, projects, and relationships full circle. Tie together loose ends. Describe how your experiences and studies benefit individuals and all humankind.

Class Selection

- ☐ Enroll in comparative religion studies. Better understand today's news events by comparing and contrasting the beliefs of the world's great religions.

- ☐ Find colleges that offer courses in the study of dreams. Look for listings in the departments of psychology, religious studies, and theology.

- ☐ Select history classes in which you can research events through the lens of conflicting religious doctrines and principles held as truth by some groups.

- ☐ Register for theology, philosophy, and ethics classes to broaden your thinking. Integrate what you learn into other coursework.

Extracurricular Activities

- ☐ Consider meeting with a spiritual advisor every four to six weeks. Describe instances of being keenly aware of the "invisible hand" of a life force, higher power, or God acting in your life. Be attentive to patterns and recurring questions.

- ☐ Get involved in campus groups and ministries to nurture your faith tradition or introduce you to new forms of spirituality.

- ☐ Opt for nontraditional school vacations. Volunteer to build a Habitat for Humanity® house, travel to a third-world nation to help in a medical clinic, clean up an inner-city neighborhood, or work with urban families to plant a neighborhood vegetable garden.

- ☐ Mentor at-risk students during the school year. Become a reading tutor for adults. Teach English to immigrant and refugee families. Record books for the blind. Serve as a camp counselor for handicapped or terminally ill children.

Applying Consistency Talents in Academics

These insights and action ideas can help you apply Consistency talents to achieve in various aspects of your academic life.

General Academic Life

- ☐ Seek professors who set the same clear expectations for everyone in the class. Make sure that you know exactly what is required to earn the grades you desire.

- ☐ Learn precisely how class participation, research, laboratory work, presentations, and examinations will be factored into your final grade for the course.

- ☐ Inform others that routines are important to your success. Explain how they lend an air of familiarity to all the coursework in your major area of study.

- ☐ Finalize your entire degree or certification plan as early in your collegiate career as possible. Each term, double-check your plan to ensure you are in compliance with graduation requirements.

- ☐ Express your belief that everyone deserves the same opportunities to earn good grades on tests, projects, research papers, or experiments. Help professors and classmates understand why you become upset when someone is given special treatment.

Study Techniques

- ☐ Anticipate what you need to do to earn the grade you want in each class. Set up and adhere to a study routine. Realize that you excel when your life has a rhythm to it.

- ☐ Make a habit of studying at the same time each day. Designate a specific study area and equip it appropriately. Replenish supplies on a specific day of the week.

- ☐ Establish predictable and uniform patterns for doing different kinds of assignments, such as writing, researching, calculating, and rehearsing speeches.

- ☐ Heighten your awareness of how much time you require to complete each assignment. Honor the ways you study best rather than mimicking those of successful classmates.

- ☐ Balance all the facts when conducting research, making a presentation, or writing a report. Seek to remove biases by being objective.

- ☐ Create study rituals that suit your thinking and learning style. Read ahead. Write down questions to which you want answers. Highlight key ideas, steps, and concepts. Take notes on note cards, in a spiral notebook, or in computer files.

Relationships

- ☐ Understand that your predictability makes you a valuable study buddy. Partner with classmates whose need for routines and processes mirror your own.

- ☐ Inform people about your need for uniformity. Help them understand how they can benefit from consistency.

- ☐ Recruit some classmates and professors with enough patience to help you recognize the need to make changes in procedures, study patterns, and routines.

Class Selection

- ☐ Identify similarities and differences in your professors' teaching styles. Choose classes taught by instructors whose approach matches your learning style.

- ☐ Avoid taking courses from professors who play favorites, change assignment requirements unexpectedly, and fail to abide by the rules they set at the start of the term.

- ☐ Make a list of courses of study that naturally incorporate routines, processes, and procedures. Consider specific science, mathematics, accounting, music, engineering, and law programs.

Extracurricular Activities

- ☐ Join clubs and teams known for their adherence to practice and rehearsal schedules.

- ☐ Help with special events that have a long history of doing things the same way from one year to the next.

- ☐ Assume accountability for monitoring compliance to rules for membership drives, fundraising, and contests.

- ☐ Volunteer to maintain the records of an organization. Ensure that accepted procedures are followed in meetings, and reports are properly submitted.

Applying Context Talents in Academics

These insights and action ideas can help you apply Context talents to achieve in various aspects of your academic life.

General Academic Life

- ☐ Associate with individuals and groups that specialize in the study of specific events, personalities, and periods in history.

- ☐ Create a historical frame of reference for whatever you study. Research political, natural, military, and religious events of that period. Delve into the lives of contemporary leaders, scientists, artists, explorers, and philosophers.

☐ Supplement required reading for classes by locating other credible sources of information. Don't let your thinking be limited to the professor's syllabus.

☐ Understand that you are attracted to institutions of learning with a rich history and a long tradition.

☐ Seek opportunities to study with reputable, recognized, and knowledgeable historians who also are master teachers.

☐ Attend lecture series in which leading figures of your time speak about their experiences in global leadership, diplomacy, military affairs, business, science, or the arts. Prepare questions to pose during the Q&A sessions or book signings.

Study Techniques

☐ Hypothesize your own theories for specific historic events. Rely on public records, surveys, correspondence, and legislation to develop a study brief.

☐ Consider your own history of test taking. Identify your best performances. Spot patterns. Prepare for today's examinations by replicating study techniques that have worked for you in the past.

☐ Overcome obstacles placed in your path by a professor by conferring with former students of this individual. Ask questions to learn from the experiences of individuals who excelled.

☐ Complement your reading and research assignments with additional sources of information, such as recorded speeches, transcripts of court proceedings, or vintage interviews with key figures and their contemporaries.

☐ Record interviews with individuals who lived through significant periods of history, such as the Great Depression, wars, terrorist attacks, political scandals, and boom times.

☐ Find photographs, paintings, drawings, blueprints, news film, videos, costumes, recipes, historical reproductions, almanacs, and costumes to bring a historic epoch to life.

Relationships

- ☐ Help people understand that knowing about their past experiences — personal and academic — will help you feel comfortable working with them on projects and in study groups.

- ☐ Decipher your methods for building a historical basis for your relationships with specific family members, friends, teammates, classmates, instructors, and coworkers.

- ☐ Ask professors about themselves on the first day of class. Inquire into their influences as children and their academic backgrounds. Read their master's theses, doctoral dissertations, books, articles, lectures, and speeches.

- ☐ Attend class reunions. Reminisce about your school days with former classmates, faculty, and administrators. Pose questions to discover what individuals have done with their lives since graduation.

Class Selection

- ☐ Choose classes taught by professors who examine cause-and-effect relationships between the actions of historic figures and the consequences they produce. Avoid history courses that require nothing beyond rote memorization of facts, names, and dates.

- ☐ Enroll in classes that allow students to study original documents and artifacts. Review the syllabus for information about field trips to museums, battlefields, archives, and theatrical productions based on historic events.

- ☐ Register for courses such as comparative religion, geography, economics, science, philosophy, and the arts to better understand the root causes of today's wars, alliances, financial policies, treaties, and trade agreements.

- ☐ Opt for classes in which you can write papers, make presentations, re-create past events, or impersonate historic figures to fulfill course requirements.

Extracurricular Activities

☐ Join a genealogy society or club. Trace your own or someone else's family tree.

☐ Serve as the historian of your fraternity, sorority, honor society, or campus organizations.

☐ Collect and archive memorabilia from events throughout the years. Volunteer to work with the campus historian to gain hands-on experience.

☐ Form a book club whose members read and then discuss autobiographies, biographies, history books, or even historic fiction.

Applying Deliberative Talents in Academics

These insights and action ideas can help you apply Deliberative talents to achieve in various aspects of your academic life.

General Academic Life

☐ Attend all lectures and class sessions — make sure you don't miss anything. Be thorough in your preparation for a class by reading ahead and reviewing class notes to avoid being caught off guard.

☐ Before visiting a professor during office hours, prepare thoroughly by making a list of items and questions you wish to discuss.

☐ Schedule regular appointments with your counselors to be well aware of your options and to make sure you are on track.

☐ When you receive a class syllabus, highlight the due dates of readings, assignments, papers, and tests. You may feel more comfortable knowing everything that will be required of you.

☐ Always be well prepared for class. You will feel more comfortable and confident talking in class when you are sure of the validity of what you have to say and the completeness of your thoughts.

☐ When taking a test, go through the questions slowly, concentrating on the ones you are more sure of first. Address the others later so that you have time to complete the exam.

Study Techniques

- ☐ Know your reading pace, and set aside plenty of time to finish reading assignments. Take notes on what you read, and study your notes for exams.

- ☐ Work extra problems just to be sure you understand the material.

- ☐ If you work best alone, study on your own before engaging in group discussions. This will allow you to reinforce what you have learned with the group, without needing to rely on the group.

- ☐ Form questions as you study, and make sure you have answers to them before taking an exam.

Relationships

- ☐ Choose friends who have academic goals similar to yours, so you reinforce one another in your serious pursuit of studying.

- ☐ Make frequent visits during office hours to develop relationships with one or two professors or teaching assistants whose advice you feel you can trust.

- ☐ When forming study groups, be selective about whom you study with. Choose responsible, serious people like yourself who will be well prepared and focus on the task at hand.

Class Selection

- ☐ Before choosing a class, look at the class syllabus, check the number of books, and learn more about the professor. Don't be caught off guard on the first day of class.

- ☐ Double check with your advisor to ensure that a class meets the requirements that you need.

- ☐ You are most comfortable in classes where you are well aware of expectations, where the discussions are serious, and where the time is used well. Before you enroll in a class, get the opinions of peers who have already taken the class.

Extracurricular Activities

☐ Look carefully at the many organizations or clubs that you might join to pinpoint those that pique your interest. Attend a couple of meetings to narrow down to one or two that seem to fit you best.

☐ Rely on your own judgment to know the types of activities that will be most enjoyable to you. Purely social activities without further purpose will most likely feel like a waste of time to you.

☐ Look for job opportunities and internships in which you will be recognized for your seriousness and your ability to raise questions about decisions that are made.

Applying Developer Talents in Academics

These insights and action ideas can help you apply Developer talents to achieve in various aspects of your academic life.

General Academic Life

☐ During lectures, take down facts that are new, enlightening, interesting, or humorous. Share your observations with others from the class.

☐ Reflect back to what you have learned from a certain professor and how that has impacted you in your life.

☐ Motivate yourself by tutoring or helping someone else in the class to understand concepts you have gained from the lecture, the reading, and the discussion.

☐ Keep an ongoing list of your key learning experiences. Track your own progress and growth.

Study Techniques

☐ Explain to a friend, fellow student, teaching assistant, or professor what you have learned from a book, lecture, or other source.

☐ Form study groups in which you can teach others as well as learn from them.

☐ Identify a few classmates on whom you can rely to be your study partners.

☐ Pretend that you are going to explain to others what you are trying to learn. This will help you retain more information and improve your comprehension.

☐ Try studying by yourself first, to understand the information, then help others if they need it. One of the best ways to reinforce your learning is to teach others.

Relationships

☐ Always have one or more mentors, and let them know what they add to your life. Consult them regularly.

☐ Help your friends choose developmental experiences.

☐ Coach friends who have a specific goal or focus in mind (such as running a marathon or losing weight). Encourage them in their progress.

Class Selection

☐ Enroll in classes with group projects, specifically those that include community service opportunities.

☐ Join tutoring and discussion groups in which you can learn from others by discussing and explaining concepts.

☐ Choose a major that highlights your ability to develop the talents of others, such as education or psychology.

☐ Choose classes with a field-studies component that involves working with people. This will provide an opportunity to see tangible growth experiences of others and observe how what you learn can be used.

Extracurricular Activities

☐ Become a tutor or a mentor. Find a role in which you can strengthen your own academic abilities while you help others improve.

☐ Start a club or community service project in which you can help other achieve.

☐ Use your ability and passion to help others by joining organizations that will allow you to exercise your talents in helping others succeed. This will allow you to feel good about what you do and learn from your experiences. For example, consider becoming a mentor or peer counselor, or join community service organizations.

☐ Consider becoming a counselor in a dorm, where you can provide an environment that facilitates the growth of other students.

Applying Discipline Talents in Academics

These insights and action ideas can help you apply Discipline talents to achieve in various aspects of your academic life.

General Academic Life

☐ Schedule all assignments, exams, and papers due for the term.

☐ Clean and organize your living space before any major assignments are due or before an examination period.

☐ If you are in a self-paced class or a class with minimal structure, develop your own structure to ensure that you meet the class requirements.

☐ Don't be afraid to color-code tasks on your calendar and your textbooks or notes. This will help you focus and prioritize what you are learning and doing.

Study Techniques

☐ Before starting papers, talk to instructors to find out what they expect and how they will grade the papers.

☐ When you come across an unfamiliar word, finish the sentence, look the word up, then reread the sentence.

- ☐ When preparing for a test, get organized. Collect all notes, have terms defined and facts highlighted and/or listed, and have possible questions available.

- ☐ When you are working on a paper, it may be best to make an outline, breaking the topic down into parts that you can work on individually.

- ☐ Use your discipline to stay ahead in reading assignments. Go over your lecture notes within 12 hours of taking them.

- ☐ Make a list of all academic tasks that you need to complete for the day. Check items off as you complete them.

Relationships

- ☐ Find some friends who are as organized as you are. You will not disappoint each other.

- ☐ Be the organizer for your friends, giving them friendly calls to remind them of when and where you are meeting for dinner, a movie, or other get-togethers.

- ☐ Delight in a partnership of planning a trip or fun event with a friend. Write down each detail so that the event will meet expectations for both of you.

Class Selection

- ☐ When choosing classes, arrange them in a way that allows studying during the times that you are more productive. Be realistic.

- ☐ Give top priority to classes that you must take for graduation requirements or your major.

- ☐ Choose professors who structure their courses and have clear expectations.

Extracurricular Activities

- ☐ Volunteer to be a timekeeper for an event. Your accuracy will be appreciated.

☐ Join a group in which you can use your organizational talents to help plan some major events, breaking down tasks to ensure that deadlines will be met.

☐ Organize a monthly or quarterly "clean up" on your living floor, in which people clear away excess papers, files, clothing, etc. Play some music, and arrange to have food brought in to make the task more appealing and fun for others.

Applying Empathy Talents in Academics

These insights and action ideas can help you apply Empathy talents to achieve in various aspects of your academic life.

General Academic Life

☐ When studying a particular author, seek personal experiences and writings that help you identify with his or her thoughts and emotions.

☐ Whenever possible, write papers about people. This activity will engage your natural ability to pinpoint individual perspectives.

☐ Keep a journal in which you reflect on what you learned from other people and their passions, fears, joys, and other emotions.

☐ You will sense when friends are academically frustrated in courses you are taking. Let them know that you realize what they are feeling, and continue to encourage and support them.

Study Techniques

☐ As soon as you have an idea, write it down, including your feelings about it.

☐ When you read, identify how you can relate the emotions of the characters to your own or those of people you know. This will make the material come alive for you and help you remember the it better.

☐ Ask yourself what the professor wants you to understand about the material, then try to master those aspects.

☐ When you're in a study group, be aware of the emotions of the other members. Help bring those feeling into the open so that others in the group can be aware of the feelings of others and you can keep your focus on the task ahead of you.

Relationships

☐ Discuss issues that are on your mind with your friends. You are usually there for them. Allow them, likewise, to be there for you. Share you feelings with them, because they may not be able to identify feelings as easily as you do.

☐ Use your Empathy talents when conflicts arise at work and other group settings.

☐ Be careful not to let those you support overwhelm you. Just as it is important you be there for your friends and family whenever they need you, it is crucial that you keep your academic goals a priority.

Class Selection

☐ Think about a major such as education or psychology, which could provide frequent opportunities to use your empathy in your future career.

☐ Choose professors who are known for their empathy as well as for their academic expertise.

☐ Classes that involve reading novels will provide you with an avenue to immerse yourself in the emotions of the characters and to learn from their approaches to situations.

Extracurricular Activities

☐ Become involved in activities, clubs, or organizations that will help you feel like you're making a difference with individuals through your empathy.

☐ Consider working with children to help them to better understand their own feelings and sort through their emotions.

☐ Position yourself as a confidante for one or two people. Many students feel overwhelmed at school; you'll understand and help them get through the difficulties they're facing.

☐ Because you're nonjudgmental and understand the feelings of individuals, you'll be a welcome addition to most groups.

Applying Focus Talents in Academics

These insights and action ideas can help you apply Focus talents to achieve in various aspects of your academic life.

General Academic Life

☐ Use your focus to link class-related assignments to the knowledge and self-management skills you'll need to be successful in your future career.

☐ Use your focus to help groups stay on track in classroom discussions or meetings.

☐ If you feel an assignment has no practical value to you, develop one that better fits your goals, and request permission from your professor to use it. Explain the potential benefits.

☐ When working with others in a small group, help them see how the pieces of a project fit together to accomplish the overall objective.

Study Techniques

☐ Before studying, list everything you'll attempt to learn during that time period.

☐ Before writing a paper, outline the main points you plan to address.

☐ Although you can concentrate for long periods of time, regulate yourself to avoid working to exhaustion.

☐ Schedule your work in a way that allows you to focus your full attention on one assignment or project at a time.

Relationships

- ☐ Talk to two or three experienced people you admire. Determine some specific strengths they possess, and ask them about their greatest talents and the knowledge and skills they acquired through the years to create these strengths.

- ☐ Choose to associate with successful people. Ask what they focused on to become successful.

- ☐ Identify an alumnus who's in a career that interests you, and spend time with that person to determine how he or she benefited from the college experience.

Class Selection

- ☐ Select classes that will help you fulfill your long-term goals.

- ☐ Select classes that have defined direction and objectives.

- ☐ Choose professors who are known for staying on track.

Extracurricular Activities

- ☐ Look for an internship in an area related to your career goals.

- ☐ Select class-related and extra-curricular activities related to your career goals.

- ☐ To build on your Focus talents and not "spread yourself too thin," be selective in the range of activities you are involved in.

Applying Futuristic Talents in Academics

These insights and action ideas can help you apply Futuristic talents to achieve in various aspects of your academic life.

General Academic Life

- ☐ Take risks to gain new insights, even if they are out of your comfort zone. Set academic goals to project yourself into a successful future.

☐ Challenge professors with your "What if?" thinking. Encourage them to project beyond to what "might be" in 10, 15, or 20 years.

☐ Know what is expected in each of your classes so you will be able to plan your college years. Visit your academic counselor regularly to keep stretching your thoughts.

☐ Associate with others who enjoy philosophizing about the future.

Study Techniques

☐ Try to truly understand what you're studying; don't just memorize. Always relate what you're studying to where you see yourself in the future.

☐ Write a description of your desired future, and post it where you will notice it frequently. Look at it often, and connect what you are learning to where you want to go.

☐ Take exams seriously and prepare thoroughly. Treat them as steps toward your future.

☐ Join a group in which you can lead others to create new visions of the future.

Relationships

☐ Talk about your goals and dreams with your friends, family, and professors. Their awareness of your objective will be a motivator.

☐ Surround yourself with people who will be instrumental in attaining your aspirations. Form strong relationships that can last a long time.

☐ Encourage younger people who are interested in the same things you enjoy.

☐ Don't let other people's negative comments about your dreams dissuade you from reaching toward them.

Class Selection

- ☐ Choose classes that will apply to your career goals.
- ☐ Pinpoint professors who are futuristic in their thinking, not those who merely maintain the status quo.
- ☐ Risk taking a class that will push you to the edge in your thinking.

Extracurricular Activities

- ☐ Join a committee that has a forward-thinking leader who can stretch you beyond day-to-day events.
- ☐ Look for internships that will challenge your thinking and help you reach beyond your current level.
- ☐ Keep others in your committee or group focused on what can be, frequently sharing the vision that you see.
- ☐ Join a group that believes that it can have a positive effect on the future.

Applying Harmony Talents in Academics

These insights and action ideas can help you apply Harmony talents to achieve in various aspects of your academic life.

General Academic Life

- ☐ Seek opinions and ideas from experts. Their insights will help you formulate your own beliefs and philosophy.
- ☐ You perform best in an environment where people listen to one another and seek to understand each other, rather than force their ideas on one another.
- ☐ You add a calmness or agreeableness to any group.
- ☐ If the professor frequently changes assignments and due dates in the middle of the term, seek reasons for the changes and share them with classmates, rather than joining the dissension of others.

Study Techniques

- ☐ Bounce ideas off others whose thinking you respect. They may be able to help you clarify your own ideas.

- ☐ Read with an open mind. Give the author a chance to explain himself or herself. Find agreement between the author's ideas and your own, and expand from there.

- ☐ When you are reading something controversial, try to find something you can agree with. Begin your study and analysis there.

- ☐ When studying in a group, help others see where their viewpoints are congruent.

Relationships

- ☐ Pick out an expert in each important area of your life and consult with them every eight to ten weeks.

- ☐ Fill a mediator role with your friends.

- ☐ Choose friends who carefully listen to one another and who are truly at ease together.

Class Selection

- ☐ You will achieve, learn a lot, and enjoy classes in which you learn practical skills and obtain practical knowledge.

- ☐ Choose classes in which there will be a minimum of controversy.

- ☐ Avoid confrontational, aggressive professors. They might make you so uncomfortable that learning in their classes will be difficult for you.

Extracurricular Activities

- ☐ Join a multicultural group, and seek the commonalities within it. You might enjoy helping the members get to know and appreciate one another.

- ☐ Volunteer at a senior citizens' home, and help them enjoy some activities together.

☐ Find a group of people who seem to truly have fun together, who have a lot in common, and who work to make one another happy and support one another. They could become your best friends.

Applying Ideation Talents in Academics

These insights and action ideas can help you apply Ideation talents to achieve in various aspects of your academic life.

General Academic Life

☐ Take on leadership positions in projects that will allow you to share several ideas and use your creativity.

☐ Take on an independent research project in which you can generate and explore numerous ideas.

☐ Work with a professor in developing a research project, and contribute your creative abilities. You probably will have many ideas to offer.

☐ Your mind may wander. You can use this to your advantage by letting your thoughts flow freely in class, as long as you think about the subject you are studying.

Study Techniques

☐ As you read an idea, use it as a stimulus for your own further thought and creativity.

☐ As you study, think of different concepts, and invent new ways to present the materials in writing or in graphics. This will invigorate your mind as well as the minds of others.

☐ Allow yourself ample time for thinking. If you rush through a reading assignment, you are less likely to be engaged with it.

☐ Brainstorm with your friends about topics you are studying. Let your mind "go wild," knowing that you can sort through the ideas later.

Relationships

☐ Surround yourself with friends who are responsive to listening as well as probing you about your ideas.

☐ Choose a mentor who has the courage to support you in your ideas and who will also challenge you to explore them even further.

☐ You love to generate ideas. Find a partner who would enjoy helping implement your ideas.

Class Selection

☐ Choose classes that involve creative projects rather than simple exams and term papers.

☐ Some classes might not seem to encourage creative expression because of their subject matter. Recognize that you can use your Ideation talents to create new and stimulating ways to learn.

☐ Select classes taught by professors who enjoy diversity of ideas.

Extracurricular Activities

☐ Join a group that values and stimulates creative ideas.

☐ Involve yourself in a project that allows you to use your creative talents, such as general writing, news magazines, newspapers, journals, graphics, or painting.

☐ Help revive a struggling group. You will have several ideas to restore life into the group. Also consider starting a totally new group and generating several ideas about projects in which it might become engaged.

Applying Includer Talents in Academics

These insights and action ideas can help you apply Includer talents to achieve in various aspects of your academic life.

General Academic Life

- ☐ In small groups in class, try to get each student to participate. Ask him or her for opinions.

- ☐ Ask shy people to walk to class with you.

- ☐ Research people of different cultures in your community. Invite some of these people to attend a community or university event with you.

- ☐ Attend lectures or speeches by guest speakers of different nationalities. Introduce yourself to others attending the session, drawing them into a conversation with you.

Study Techniques

- ☐ Study with other people. If someone in the group is not talking, try to bring him or her into the conversation.

- ☐ Invite someone who is shy but intelligent to study with you.

- ☐ Start a small study group of people who seem more hesitant to talk, and include a couple of more verbal people as well.

- ☐ Search out books on the culture of a prominent ethnic group in your community. Use your new information to help include some people of this culture in activities in which you participate.

Relationships

- ☐ Expand your relationships to have a diverse group of friends with whom you participate in activities.

- ☐ You can adjust to many types of people and help them feel welcome. Invite others to your social activities.

- ☐ Welcome new students to your dorm or living space. Many people assume that others will just make themselves at home. You help them feel a part of the group.

Class Selection

☐ Sign up for classes in which you will learn more about the uniqueness of particular groups of people. Use this information to help them feel included.

☐ Select classes in which the professor tries to involve each student.

☐ Select classes that promote diversity.

Extracurricular Activities

☐ Your ability to help others feel like part of the group will make you a valuable member of student organizations and service groups.

☐ Help tutor those who do not have the social or economic privileges you have. Develop or participate in programs that promote diversity.

☐ Volunteer to help with a cause such as Special Olympics.

Applying Individualization Talents in Academics

These insights and action ideas can help you apply Individualization talents to achieve in various aspects of your academic life.

General Academic Life

☐ Build on your curiosity about people by observing the different ways in which people learn and process information.

☐ Read, read, read about people. Their uniqueness fascinates you.

☐ Constantly observe those around you, seeing how your talents make you similar to each other, yet different.

☐ Study various cultures. Their uniqueness will intrigue you.

Study Techniques

☐ Establish a study group with people who possess a wide variety of talents and perspectives, thereby expanding your own horizons and viewpoints.

☐ As you read a novel, take notes about how the author vividly sets up the uniqueness of each character.

☐ Note how your style of learning, studying, writing papers, and taking tests compares to others. You will learn about some of the natural differences between people.

☐ As you read about well known people, make a chart listing specific differences among them. This will hone your observation talents.

Relationships

☐ See the great talents in people, and encourage people to follow their own dreams. Help them understand and maximize the power of their talents.

☐ Help your friends and classmates see and appreciate the and uniqueness in each other.

☐ Create small support systems, using your Individualization talents to determine who might benefit from another's insights.

Class Selection

☐ Enroll in classes about people, such as literature, sociology, and psychology.

☐ Choose classes that promote discussion, bringing out varying beliefs from students.

☐ Choose professors who allow students to make choices regarding their own learning.

Extracurricular Activities

☐ Be a mentor. You will pinpoint people's unique qualities and encourage them to follow their own paths.

☐ Seek peer-counseling opportunities that make use of your ability to know each person as an individual.

☐ Keep a journal that includes specific observations about individual people. Write some feature articles about people on campus for the school newspaper.

Applying Input Talents in Academics

These insights and action ideas can help you apply Input talents to achieve in various aspects of your academic life.

General Academic Life

☐ Save all notes and books from previous classes to create a personal library.

☐ Schedule time for seeking information that goes beyond what is required for your classes. The library and the Internet will be valuable in your search.

☐ You enjoy gathering information, possible even from reading a dictionary or encyclopedia.

☐ Start a filing system for interesting and potentially useful articles you have read.

Study Techniques

☐ Give yourself research deadlines within your overall timelines for completing papers. Without them, you might continue to read and read, never feeling like you have enough information.

☐ To continue making progress and stay on track while doing required work, put sticky notes on areas you wish to go back and look at.

☐ Prioritize the most critical information to study. Otherwise, you might become distracted by other information that fascinates you but is not as relevant.

Relationships

☐ Share your information with friends. Determine who would be interested in each bit of information, rather than giving all information to everyone.

☐ Seek out professors who would be interested in knowing what you are learning and will find it stimulating to hear about the questions you are generating through your investigations.

☐ Be aware that the more you know, the more likely it is that others will seek you out for information and see you as highly credible.

Class Selection

☐ Select classes taught by professors who are well read and who keep up to date on the latest research in their fields.

☐ Select classes that help you increase your general knowledge base. That would include classes in which research is valued.

☐ Select classes in which class discussion is valued and in which you can share your ideas and the information that you have gleaned.

Extracurricular Activities

☐ Join groups in which you can use your knowledge, such as community discussion groups, book clubs, and pre-law society mock trial groups.

☐ Become involved in extracurricular activities that further your learning, such as science clubs, language clubs, or literary organizations.

☐ Study about fascinating places to travel. Gather information, and go!

Applying Intellection Talents in Academics

These insights and action ideas can help you apply Intellection talents to achieve in various aspects of your academic life.

General Academic Life

☐ Ask questions and seek answers in discussions and lectures.

☐ Research subjects that interest and intrigue you.

☐ Contemplate academic goals and endeavors.

☐ Make your education even more effective by following your intellectual curiosity. As you allow yourself to ask the questions that naturally come to you, you will refine your approach to learning and studying.

Study Techniques

- ☐ Take time to think and plan before writing a paper or performing an assignment.
- ☐ Study to understand and learn, not just to memorize.
- ☐ Take part in study groups that allow you to verbalize and further define your thoughts.
- ☐ Practice presenting ideas that matter to you.

Relationships

- ☐ Get to know your professors, and engage them in discussions.
- ☐ Try to meet people who share the same interests, and create intellectual conversations with them.
- ☐ Surround yourself with intellectually stimulating people, and confidently converse with them. You can contribute to their lives as well as they can to yours.

Class Selection

- ☐ Take classes that promote intellectual and analytical thought.
- ☐ Choose professors whose reputations indicate that they demand careful thinking.
- ☐ Study course syllabi to know how much thinking you might have an opportunity to do.

Extracurricular Activities

- ☐ Join clubs that allow you to be part of stimulating conversations.
- ☐ Read and collect books that pique your curiosity.
- ☐ Attend conferences and debates about the subjects in which you are most interested.

Applying Learner Talents in Academics

These insights and action ideas can help you apply Learner talents to achieve in various aspects of your academic life.

General Academic Life

☐ Keep a journal in which you reflect on what you learned from your classes and other experiences.

☐ Read outside material that is related to your courses. This approach will not only impress the professor; it also will help you develop a better understanding of the subject.

☐ Exceed expectations. Do more than the syllabus requires of you.

☐ Look at every situation as a possible learning experience. This approach will help you become aware of what you do well and where you need help.

☐ Always ask, "What did I learn from this?"

Study Techniques

☐ Join study groups that challenge you.

☐ Study in an environment that allows you to get into a "study mood." This approach allow you to get the most out of your studies.

☐ Figure out questions that will be asked, and practice answering them in preparation for discussions and exams.

Relationships

☐ Identify classmates who share your thirst for knowledge, and get to know them.

☐ Have lots of conversations on subjects you are passionate about with people who are interested in learning.

☐ Build relationships with those from whom you want to learn.

Class Selection

☐ Choose challenging courses that will broaden your knowledge base in important areas.

☐ Enroll in college honors and departmental honors classes.

Extracurricular Activities

☐ Choose on-campus jobs that will provide learning experiences, such as working as a professor's assistant.

☐ Don't restrict your learning experiences to the classroom. Engage in activities in which you can expand your knowledge about subject that interest you most.

☐ Find opportunities to work with faculty and teaching assistants to make your college experience more meaningful. It will deepen your understanding of intellectual topics, concepts, and principles.

Applying Maximizer Talents in Academics

These insights and action ideas can help you apply Maximizer talents to achieve in various aspects of your academic life.

General Academic Life

☐ Consider specialized programs that allow you to refine your talents.

☐ Find mentors — and be one.

☐ Study success. Find out what made famous scientists, historic figures, and great innovators successful. The greatest outcome of college can be your insights into what makes people, societies, cultures, and groups successful.

☐ Select a college or university that offers leadership opportunities in which you can maximize the talents of others.

Maximizer in Academics

Study Techniques

☐ Read wherever you feel most comfortable — the library, the coffee shop, or home.

☐ Discover your best way to learn, and stick to it.

☐ Determine ways to manage any weaknesses in your study habits.

☐ Study the most of what you do the best.

Relationships

☐ Make a point of helping your friends use their greatest talents to the fullest.

☐ Help your friends recognize the talents and strengths in others.

☐ Associate with people who appreciate your talents as well as their own.

☐ Meet regularly with mentors and role models for insight, advice, and inspiration.

Class Selection

☐ Pick elective courses that will provide opportunities to develop new strengths and hone your existing strengths.

☐ Choose your major on the basis of your greatest talents and your personal mission. In what area of study do you have the greatest potential for strengths?

☐ Seek classes taught by professors whose teaching styles best match the way you learn.

Extracurricular Activities

☐ Find an internship or a job in which you can apply your greatest talents and your existing strengths.

☐ Involve yourself in mentoring or tutoring.

☐ Join organizations that have missions related to development.

Applying Positivity Talents in Academics

These insights and action ideas can help you apply Positivity talents to achieve in various aspects of your academic life.

General Academic Life

- ☐ Help make learning fun.
- ☐ Share praise when appropriate.
- ☐ Help classmates laugh and relax when needed.
- ☐ Contribute to exciting class discussions.

Study Techniques

- ☐ Invite study partners who are as upbeat as you.
- ☐ Encourage others to enjoy their assignments.
- ☐ Think of fun, even silly, ways to remember things.
- ☐ Make learning fun for yourself and others by throwing study parties.

Relationships

- ☐ Express your positive attitudes about life to others.
- ☐ Transfer your energy into everything that you do.
- ☐ Let positive emotions reign, and avoid those who are guided by negative, destructive, and defeating attitudes and practices.
- ☐ Choose friends who love life as much as you do.

Class Selection

- ☐ Take classes that you find exciting and meaningful.
- ☐ Select courses led by professors who have positive approaches.
- ☐ Investigate what others with a lot of positivity say about the courses you are considering.

Extracurricular Activities

☐ Play or support team sports in which can you enjoy cheering others on.

☐ Actively seek out extracurricular activities that might be fun.

☐ Pump energy into clubs you join.

Applying Relator Talents in Academics

These insights and action ideas can help you apply Relator talents to achieve in various aspects of your academic life.

General Academic Life

☐ Create various lines of communication with friends in your classes, such as verbal, phone, and e-mail, and help each other when one of you has to miss a class.

☐ Seek out advisors, counselors, and professors who demonstrate genuine interest in you as a person.

☐ Seek out fellow students with whom you can play a mutual tutoring, learning assistance, and support role.

Study Techniques

☐ Form study groups for midterms and exams with close friends.

☐ Discuss class lectures with friends.

☐ Study with friends who have goals similar to yours.

☐ To increase your comprehension of reading materials, share what you have learned with friends.

Relationships

☐ Share knowledge with others and build a support network.

☐ Become a mentor and always have a mentor.

☐ Get to know professors who take an interest in you. Their involvement in your college experience will create a sense of belonging and stimulate your intellectual development as well as your academic achievement.

☐ Develop a college lifestyle through which you share your academic progress and performance with people who care about you, both inside and outside the college environment.

Class Selection

☐ Do your best to meet the professors who teach the classes you are considering.

☐ Choose classes that friends are taking. Your relationships with them will heighten your engagement in the classes.

☐ Select classes that encourage friendships and belonging.

Extracurricular Activities

☐ Become involved in campus organizations that foster friendships.

☐ Join organizations that your friends and you have agreed upon.

☐ Consider community and humanitarian work that you can rally your close friends to be a part of too.

Applying Responsibility Talents in Academics

These insights and action ideas can help you apply Responsibility talents to achieve in various aspects of your academic life.

General Academic Life

☐ Prepare for the term by listing the dates of all tests, projects, and papers.

☐ Ask professors and successful students to show you what an "A" paper and an "A" essay look like.

☐ Think about what it would mean to be a truly responsible student. Work toward that standard in a progressive manner, taking one step at a time.

☐ Strive to always work ahead. Read ahead and work problems before the professor has presented them in class.

Study Techniques

- ☐ Discover what "doing it right" means to each of your professors.
- ☐ Schedule specific study times for each of your classes, and assume full responsibility for investing the necessary time, talents, and effort.
- ☐ As you do your reading assignments, highlight the key vocabulary words, main ideas, and characters.
- ☐ Make choices about class assignments as soon as possible.

Relationships

- ☐ Choose friends you trust.
- ☐ Find a mentor.
- ☐ Consider having a circle of friends who are older than you.

Class Selection

- ☐ Choose core classes or those required by your major first.
- ☐ Select professors you trust.
- ☐ Opt for courses in which you have choices to make about your learning.

Extracurricular Activities

- ☐ Wisely consider how much time you can devote to clubs and activities.
- ☐ Run for an office only if you have the capacity to fulfill it as you would like.
- ☐ Select organizations that stand for the same values you do.

Applying Restorative Talents in Academics

These insights and action ideas can help you apply Restorative talents to achieve in various aspects of your academic life.

General Academic Life

☐ Read the syllabus when you get it, and attack assignments or areas that you consider problematic.

☐ Do not let an unexpectedly low grade defeat your spirits. Learn how to more effectively apply your greatest talents.

☐ Think about school as a way to improve yourself. You will increase your motivation, particularly if you reflect on your progress.

Study Techniques

☐ Make a list of ways in which you can apply your most powerful talents to improve in each class.

☐ Ask your professors what your weaknesses are, and create support systems or complementary partnerships through which you can manage them.

☐ Research every missed test question to determine your gaps in knowledge, and fill those gaps.

Relationships

☐ Let others know that you enjoy fixing their problems.

☐ Ask friends for honest feedback about your weaknesses.

☐ Build relationships with people who appreciate your ability to help them identify problems.

Class Selection

☐ Select classes that emphasize case solutions.

☐ Select classes in which you learn to solve problems.

☐ Choose classes led by a professor who wants to fix things.

Extracurricular Activities

☐ Raise money for the disadvantaged.

☐ Organize a club that tackles and solves social issues on campus.

☐ Join an organization in which you can restore something to its original condition.

Applying Self-Assurance Talents in Academics

These insights and action ideas can help you apply Self-Assurance talents to achieve in various aspects of your academic life.

General Academic Life

☐ Ensure that you are completely in control of your grades. Gain a clear understanding of what is expected and how meet those expectations.

☐ Always strive to become a better student. Stick with what is working for you and continue to build on your most powerful talents.

☐ Be confident in your abilities to understand and learn material.

☐ Register for classes that excite you.

Study Techniques

☐ Overstudy. Do more than you need to do.

☐ Have confidence in your best ways to learn.

☐ Study your greatest talents, and recognize the many ways in which you can achieve through them.

☐ Enjoy the risks you take in your approach to studying.

Relationships

☐ Get to know your professors and teaching assistants. This approach will help you stay in control of your learning.

☐ Build a potentially lifetime friendship with an instructor.

☐ Seek people who appreciate your self-confidence.

Class Selection

☐ Choose classes that you will find challenging and intriguing.

☐ Select classes that play to your strengths and greatest talents.

☐ Choose classes in which you can achieve major successes.

Extracurricular Activities

☐ Seek a leadership position in an organization that addresses issues important to you. You know you can make an important difference in these areas.

☐ Join clubs that will "stretch" your talents and your horizons. Dare to tackle the unfamiliar.

☐ Consider a semester abroad. Your Self-Assurance talents will help you maneuver through a culture that is quite different from your own.

Applying Significance Talents in Academics

These insights and action ideas can help you apply Significance talents to achieve in various aspects of your academic life.

General Academic Life

☐ Think about why a particular class is important to your future.

☐ Identify three of your personal goals and connect them to your academic life.

☐ Take control of your life, beginning with your education.

☐ Create a list of goals that will bring you great satisfaction in your personal life. Then consider how college can help you reach those goals.

Study Techniques

☐ Take a leadership role in a study group.

☐ Choose to study with other hard-charging classmates.

☐ Establish relationships with your professors so they know who you are and of your interest in achieving.

Relationships

- ☐ Associate with professors and students whose interests and goals are similar to your own.

- ☐ You want people to know who you are. Become friends with people in your classes by initiating conversations with them.

- ☐ You want people to appreciate your work, but if appreciation is not shown, don't give up. Work even harder.

Class Selection

- ☐ Choose classes that offer you some independence.

- ☐ Select classes relevant to your goals and desires.

- ☐ Select classes in which you can be highly successful.

Extracurricular Activities

- ☐ Take part in activities that display and make use of your confidence — make public appearances, climb mountains.

- ☐ Run for an elected office.

Applying Strategic Talents in Academics

These insights and action ideas can help you apply Strategic talents to achieve in various aspects of your academic life.

General Academic Life

- ☐ Don't be afraid to be different. Discuss with professors the various approaches you can take to tackle an assignment.

- ☐ Participate in research, or develop your own research project.

- ☐ Search for ways to express your creative thinking.

- ☐ Opt for classes that encourage discussion and creative solutions.

Study Techniques

- ☐ Reflect and write down your ideas for possible solutions to problems.

- [ ] In group settings, work with others to generate new ideas or clarify your own.

- [ ] Be creative in your studying. Make up games or develop mnemonic devices and anecdotes to relate information.

- [ ] Do more than is expected. It is not difficult for you to expand on an idea, and you will learn more about the subject.

Relationships

- [ ] Seek a leadership role in a group. You see the path to success more clearly than many.

- [ ] As you seek to achieve your leadership goals, always have your followers in mind.

- [ ] Encourage friends to call on you to devise the best way to achieve their goals.

Class Selection

- [ ] Consider taking an independent-study class. Your Strategic talents can help you work on your own.

- [ ] Consider elective classes with subject matter that lends itself to strategic thinking, like engineering or marketing.

- [ ] Choose classes that emphasize alternative ideas or solutions.

Extracurricular Activities

- [ ] Consider running for an elected office, and confidently state your ideas.

- [ ] Participate in cultural activities and exchanges to better understand the world around you.

- [ ] Find organizations that need your planning abilities.

Applying Woo Talents in Academics

These insights and action ideas can help you apply Woo talents to achieve in various aspects of your academic life.

General Academic Life

☐ Make classroom discussions fun by using words that catch the attention of others.

☐ Meet and greet the people in your classes.

☐ Use your charm when asking difficult questions in class.

Study Techniques

☐ Study in places where there are many people, like the library or an off-campus bookstore.

☐ Block off time for studying and reading with others.

☐ Connect reading material to people you have met. This helps you get involved in the reading and not become bored, and you will better remember what you read and generate more insights.

☐ Create a study group of people you do not know yet.

Relationships

☐ Schedule a time (at least twice a quarter) to visit your professors during office hours. Have them get to know you by name.

☐ Start a conversation with your classmates to identify students with whom you can work, learn, and study.

☐ Use your networking strengths every way you can. Prepare for class, exams, discussions, and papers with other people.

☐ Join social groups and study groups.

Class Selection

☐ Try to meet the professors before choosing classes.

☐ Choose classes that offer opportunities to meet lots of people.

☐ Ask fellow students for their opinions about classes you are considering.

Extracurricular Activities

☐ Get involved in an activity or group that gives you the opportunity to connect with different people.

☐ Balance your academics with extracurricular activities to keep yourself involved with people.

☐ Run for an elected office. A person with exceptional Woo talents can quickly connect with people and create positive reactions.

☐ Chair large social events. Turn on your charm to engage others.

Chapter VIII

DEVELOPING LEADERSHIP
STRENGTHS IN COLLEGE

For many people, college is a stepping-stone to careers in which they will be leaders. They might hope to lead in a classroom, a courtroom, a corporation, a community, a hospital, an agency, a ministry, or their own business. Also, many college graduates will move into supervisory roles. Both of these facts point to the importance of learning about effective leadership.

All of the talents in the themes measured by the Clifton StrengthsFinder can be applied to leadership roles and responsibilities. Therefore, if you assume any leadership roles in college, you will have opportunities to develop leadership strengths.

Take mentoring, for example. Often, when a college student is mentored by a professor or staff member on campus, that student's intellectual and personal development increases significantly. Even fellow students, especially those who are a year or two ahead of you, can be very helpful as mentors. You would probably find it very beneficial to have a peer with whom you can continually reflect on your college experience.

But *being* a mentor is just as important as *having* a mentor. If you truly want to develop leadership strengths, you must seek out people to help you — and find people who would benefit from what you have learned.

The college experience provides a magnificent opportunity to develop leadership strengths. The key is to be intentional. Talents within each and every one of your Signature Themes can be applied in college, and many can be applied in multiple leadership functions. Look for every opportunity to refine your greatest talents in leadership roles.

In our work with thousands of college students, we have identified several ways in which you can intentionally develop leadership strengths in college. We present these suggestions to stimulate your thinking.

There certainly are many more ways to use the college experience to build leadership strengths. Let your imagination devise the approach and the activities that are best for you.

1. Leadership development and the college experience in general

Pay particular attention to when and how you influence others and how you are able to rally others to make changes. Conversely, note when and how others influence you and rally you to make changes.

2. Leadership development and the classroom experience

Classes and the work of instructors in the classroom provide wonderful opportunities to learn about leadership. Because learning always involves changing — and because leadership is designed to produce measurable change — you will want to note when and how instructors influence students to change. Here are some questions that will stimulate your thinking as you learn about leadership from observing and reflecting on the work of educators as leaders.

- What are the differences between effective and ineffective instructors?

- What talents do the best instructors seem to have?

- How do the best instructors interact with students?

- How do the best instructors organize lessons and classroom activities?

- How do the most effective instructors persuade others?

- How do effective instructors use their talents when they teach and interact with students?

- Which talents do you have in common with the most effective instructors?

3. Leadership development and class selection

Almost all the classes in a field of study can provide valuable insights for the learner who intentionally wants to develop leadership strengths. Here are some examples:

- any classes in communication studies or speech

- any classes in leadership studies or management

- almost all classes in sociology or social psychology

- most classes in organizational development, organizational psychology, and community development

- humanities classes that focus on rhetoric and persuasion

- philosophy classes in argumentation and logical reasoning

- mathematical reasoning and patterns in scientific problem-solving classes most classes in political science

- many classes in cultural anthropology

- many classes in ethnic and cross-cultural studies

- history and other social science classes that focus on the dynamics of change and/or the influence of particular leaders in the change process

4. Leadership development in class assignments and independent studies

Make class assignments work for you by applying them to the study of leaders and leadership. We recommend you focus your studies on the best leaders and the reasons for their outstanding performances. You may be able to do library research and study historical or current leaders. You might even conduct your own investigations of the best leaders you know or those who are superior in a particular field. As you study, here are some questions to consider. What is it that makes these leaders so effective? What are their greatest talents? In what environment and with what groups of people do leaders with certain talents seem to be most effective?

5. Leadership development in athletics

On the most basic level, athletics can help you understand a lot about leadership and the concept of talents and strengths. You also learn about how you need different types of talent to play different kinds of sports and positions. There's also the whole challenge of developing strengths and the taking the right attitudes.

Additional insights about leadership can be gained from asking the following questions about sports and athletic competition. What makes a great coach? How do effective coaches work with their players?

- What are effective coaches doing during practice and during a game?

- What are the most important elements of preparation?

- What are the most important things to do and not do during training?

- What is the best way to learn a new approach, a new play, or new moves?

- What is involved in changing old habits and developing new ones?

- What are the best ways to formulate goals?

- How can you best develop a team and "team spirit"?

- How can you best deal with discouragements, injuries, and setbacks?

- What are the most effective ways to maintain motivation?

6. Leadership development through internships and experiential education opportunities

Most colleges and universities offer internships in which you can work with professionals in a given field. These provide up-close and personal looks at how leadership works in real life. Even if the internship isn't the most positive experience, you can learn what not to do when you are a leader. Also, you may have opportunities to perform several other leadership functions through your internship or experiential education opportunity.

7. Leadership development in study groups

As you work with other students in study groups, use your various talents to help yourself and others learn. For example, an effective leader helps others use their talents to help the group function better and to move toward a desired goal. Likewise, consider the talents of other members of your study group, and try to allocate the tasks of the study group according to those talents.

As you use study groups to develop leadership strengths, look for every opportunity to help other people learn more about their most natural talents. In the process, you will be learning more about your own.

8. Leadership development through student organizations

Student clubs, organizations, and service projects provide some of the best leadership development opportunities available on campus. But this also presents a massive challenge because students have multiple commitments and competing priorities, and their work in student organizations is almost exclusively unpaid. However, students who meet the challenge of providing appropriate attention to each of their responsibilities receive excellent opportunities to develop leadership strengths.

9. Leadership development through employment experience

Nearly every college student works to pay for some or all of his or her college and living expenses. But rather than considering employment as only a job for earning money, try to make it a learning experience through which you can develop leadership talents.

Managing others can be one of the most important aspects of leadership. From the strengths perspective, managers will be most effective if they capitalize on their greatest talents and consciously use them as they manage others.

The best management approaches take into account the talents of both the manager and those who are managed. One of Gallup's bestselling books, *Now, Discover Your Strengths*, offers specific strategies for how a manager can use his or her talents to best manage others. The same book describes how to take into account the individual talents of those who are being managed.

Armed with the knowledge contained in *Now, Discover Your Strengths*, you'll be able to see when people are and are not using their talents in management, and you can begin thinking about how you can best manage others by most effectively using your own talents.

10. Other opportunities for leadership development within the college experience

In addition to the opportunities listed above, the college experience provides countless opportunities to develop your leadership abilities. For example, most colleges provide opportunities for students to become involved in musical performances, drama, theater, and other artistic modes of expression.

Developing leadership strengths is a process that begins with who you are, then moves to what you do. Here are principles that you can follow to become a person who leads on the basis of your talents.

- Realize that you do not need to be in a formal leadership role to provide valuable leadership. Identify the specific leadership tasks that you can perform with strength, and take them on when the opportunity arises.

- Lead with your talents as you work in groups to help them reach goals.

- Pay close attention to others in the organization, and try to identify their most powerful talents.

- Encourage others in the organization by helping them see the positive contributions they are making as they use their talents productively.

- Create opportunities for others to develop and use their talents — opportunities to do what they naturally do best.

- Become clear about your personal goals, and help the members of the organization focus on the goals they want to accomplish.

This aspect of becoming a strengths-based leader cannot be emphasized enough: Be intentional. Purposely look at each college experience in terms of learning something about how to be a leader. Whether you are a leader or a follower doesn't matter. In either role, you can learn something about leadership.

Chapter IX

BECOMING YOUR OWN BEST
EDUCATOR AND LEARNER

For more than 30 years, Professor Robert Rosenthal has conducted experiments on the power of expectations to influence performance and intellectual competence. Here is a summary of one of his most famous experiments:

Oak School is a public elementary school with approximately 650 students. At the beginning of one school year, all of the students were pre-tested with a standard test of intelligence. The teachers were told that the test could predict "intellectual blooming" and also predict which students would soon experience "spurts" of intellectual development.

About 20% of the Oak School students were identified as "potential bloomers." Each of the 18 teachers was given the names of those "special" students in his or her class who would show dramatic intellectual growth in the academic year ahead. These predictions were allegedly made on the basis of these "special" students' scores on the test for potential "academic blooming."

However, the "special" students had actually been chosen randomly. The difference between them and the "ordinary" students was only in the minds of the teachers.

All of the Oak School students were retested with the same intelligence test after one semester and again at the end of the year.

When the test scores of the "special" students and the "ordinary" students were calculated, both groups showed an improvement in total I.Q., verbal I.Q., and reasoning I.Q. But when the two groups were compared, 47% of the "special" students had gained 20 or more total I.Q. points, while only 19% of the "ordinary" students gained 20 or more total I.Q. points.

The Power of Expectations

Research by Dr. Rosenthal and others clearly indicates that our expectations have a powerful effect on ourselves and others. These expectations influence our actions, attitudes, motivation, and perseverance. In fact, they influence every aspect of achieving, including whether or not we will even enter into activities where we can achieve excellence. Because of the critical importance of expectations, we want you to consider these questions.

1. Why do you think the "special" students at Oak School performed so well?

2. If these "special" students had the ability to achieve such excellence all along, why hadn't they performed as well before?

3. If these teachers were able to promote achievement among "special" students at this level, what could have happened if they had realized that *all* of their students were special?

4. Are there certain people whom you think are special? If so, what expectations do you have of them?

5. In what ways do your expectations of these special people influence their achievements and performance?

6. In what ways do you think you are special and have real potential for blossoming?

7. In what ways are your self-expectations encouraging your achievements and performance?

The Missed Opportunities Revealed by Rosenthal's Research

Dr. Rosenthal's research has been very helpful in improving how teachers are trained and the expectations they have of themselves, their roles, and their interactions with students. But this research also shines a light on what we believe is a series of key points.

The first key point is that the "special" students always had the ability to blossom, but no one ever brought that ability to the surface. If the "special" students wouldn't have had the ability before the school year began, no amount of good teaching could have produced results that were more than double what the "ordinary" students achieved.

The second key point is that it took fraudulent information from a researcher to get the teachers to help their students blossom. The teachers already had the ability to produce academic achievements among their students. The teachers were not given any different curriculum, nor were they given any additional teaching methods, training, or new technology. Sadly, although these teachers already had within them the ability to inspire students to blossom, they had not put that ability to use.

The third key point revealed by Rosenthal's research was that the underperformance by both the students and the teachers stemmed from the teachers' "ordinary" expectations of their "ordinary" students. Just think about all of the students at Oak School who did not achieve their potential because their teachers didn't see them as being anything special. The sad thing about this is that normal expectations are usually low.

Some students experience only negative expectations every day. Some of these negative expectations are placed arbitrarily on young people simply because of how they look, their gender, socio-economic status, or ethnicity.

A great deal of research is now being conducted about the topic of "stereotype threat." This research shows that when people are in an environment where they perceive that they are being stereotyped with negative expectations about their abilities to perform, their performances confirm the negative expectations, like self-fulfilling prophecies. Research by Stanford University Professor Claude Steele and others reveals that environmental expectations form and reinforce self-expectations that directly influence performance.

What Really Happened in the Rosenthal Studies of Expectations?

The teachers in Rosenthal's study acted differently toward the "special" students, both in how they taught and in how they interacted with these students. In essence, the experimenters had changed the teachers' approaches to their students by manipulating the teachers' perceptions of the students.

More than 400 studies have been conducted to document the powerful effects of expectations. Drs. Rosenthal and Monica Harris have synthesized the research findings from many of these studies to determine exactly what teachers do when they are given more favorable information about certain "high potential" students. What follows is a list of the teachers' behaviors toward the students who they were told had special abilities and special potential for achieving.

1. Teachers expressed more positive attitudes, behaviors, and emotional warmth toward the "special" students.

2. Teachers more frequently acknowledged, applied, and/or summarized what the "special" students had to say.

3. Teachers taught the "special" students more challenging material than they presented to the "normal" students.

4. Teachers interacted with the "special" students more frequently about both academic and nonacademic topics.

5. Teachers made eye contact with the "special" students more frequently.

6. Teachers asked the "special" students more questions.

7. Teachers gave the "special" students more positive feedback and praise.

A Radical Idea: Become Your Own Best Teacher

Dr. Winston C. Doby has conceptualized a learning system based on a group of beliefs found among outstanding learners. In particular, he has found that top learners believe they are their own best teachers and take personal responsibility for their own learning.

Quite often, an ineffective relationship between a teacher and a learner is the result of miscommunication or a lack of communication. But when you are your own teacher and your own learner, there is very little chance of these communication problems. Your inner dialogue and your clear self-awareness are primary reasons why you can be your own best teacher and your own best learner. Also, the basis for your positive expectations about yourself is neither random nor fraudulent. You know you have talents of great value.

We challenge you to be at least as good with your "student within" as the teachers in Rosenthal's study were with their special students.

Putting this in practical terms, consider doing the following.

1. Express positive attitudes toward yourself as a learner.

2. Use challenging material to encourage growth.

3. Give positive feedback and praise to your learner within.

Know this: If you want to achieve excellence in education, you must assume the responsibility of being your own best teacher and your own best learner.

Perception of Talent

Perception of talent plays an extremely influential role in a person's motivation to achieve.

When people perceive that they have minimal talent, they usually avoid any activity that may reveal that lack of talent. Procrastination is a typical manifestation of a perceived lack of talent. It's like a game in which you do everything at the last minute so that if you don't succeed, you can blame the failure on a lack of time rather than a lack of talent.

In our experience, most people perceive that they have little talent, if any at all. And even when people are aware of their talents, they aren't very clear about the nature of their talents or what to do with them. They also tend to believe that their talents have limited uses and are applicable in only one or two areas.

People may even totally misperceive a powerful talent, thinking it is a weakness.

We emphasize the perception of talent because when people decide to enter or avoid an achievement activity, they are not making their decision based on what their talents really are or what they are actually capable of doing through them. They make their achievement or avoidance decision on the basis of their perception of their talents.

Becoming Your Own Best Educator and Learner

It's been said that there's no lasting change without a change of identity. Your identity is your perception of who you are, and it forms the boundaries of what you attempt to do. People seldom undertake tasks beyond their perception of who they are and what they can do.

Earlier in this chapter, we presented the radical idea that you are your own best teacher. This idea by Dr. Doby is similar to Parker Palmer's concept of the educator within. We would like to take these ideas to a higher level and encourage you to pursue a greater identity: *You are your own best educator and learner.*

Never forget that we live in a fast-moving world in which only three things are certain: (1) rapid change, (2) continuing knowledge explosion, and (3) increasingly complex relationships that are more difficult to maintain. To cope, let alone achieve in this environment, everyone faces the possibility of becoming "obsolete" if they don't keep learning.

Lifelong learning isn't a luxury; it's a necessity. Being a lifelong learner is your only way of coping with rapid change, knowledge explosion, and complex relationships. No matter what field you enter, you must forever be a learner, or you will be left behind.

Chapter X

STRENGTHS AND CAREER PLANNING

Mark Twain told the story of a man who searched his whole life for the world's greatest general. When the man died, he arrived in heaven and walked up to St. Peter and said, "I'm looking for the world's greatest general."

St. Peter replied, "I know. We've been expecting you, and I have good news. If you will look right over there, you will see the world's greatest general."

The older man excitedly looked over and said, "That's not the world's greatest general. That man was a cobbler on Main Street in my hometown." St. Peter responded, "But had he been a general, he would have been the greatest general ever."

This story is not meant to demean cobblers at all. The work of a cobbler is meaningful and requires very special talents. But the story does raise some fundamental questions: Did the cobbler know what he had the potential to do? Did he know that he had the talent to be the world's greatest general? Did anyone try to convince him that he could be destined for greatness?

Twain's tale points to a painful truth that's echoed in the words of Oliver Wendell Holmes: "Most people go to their graves with their music still inside them." There are plenty of perfectly good cobblers out there who could have been great generals, given the opportunity or encouragement. Maybe, given the choice, they would still have chosen to be cobblers. But they also could have pursued completely different, perhaps historic, careers.

Give this tale some thought when planning your own career. We want the music that is inside you to be heard!

It's a Question of Fit

The Chinese philosopher Confucius had it right 2,500 years ago: "Choose a job you love, and you will never have to work a day in your life." We spend half our waking hours at work — 90,000 hours of our lives, if we work from college graduation to retirement at age 65. That's a lot of time that can be spent either doing something you love — and marveling at the fact that you're getting paid for it — or dreading getting up every morning. In the United States, only 13% of workers say they find their work meaningful, and a mere 20% think they're in jobs that are using their talents (Miller, 1999). If you're like us, you want to be counted among the 1 in 5 that enjoys going to work on Monday morning.

From childhood on, your parents, teachers, and well-meaning friends and relatives have been asking you, "What do you want to be when you grow up?" The pressure to make the right choice only intensifies as you head to college. Many people think you should have it figured out by the time you arrive on campus. Yet the reality is that choosing a career is a daunting task, and you're not alone if you struggle with it. Anywhere from 60 to 85% of entering college students change their major at least once. So it's important to recognize that this is a big deal that people struggle with and that may take some time to figure out. Some avoid it as long as possible, and others take the easy road and choose whatever career they think their parents might like them to pursue.

Read just about any book on career choice and you'll find a theme that runs through them all: Choosing a career is all about the right fit. When you find a career that fits you, work doesn't seem so much like work anymore; work allows you to express the essence of who you are and brings you joy. Thomas Edison claimed, "I never did a day's work in my life. It was all fun."

Interestingly, he was also the one who said, "Genius is one percent inspiration and ninety-nine percent perspiration." Interviews with people in their seventies and eighties have revealed that those who had a passion for their work were also the ones who felt their lives were most fulfilling and meaningful (Leider & Shapiro, 2001). And at the end of life, that's what counts: looking back on a life well-lived and feeling that you made a difference.

Because this is an issue of fit, one question that comes to mind is whether there's one perfect fit, one right career choice. We might like to think that there is some career out there that will be just right. But we don't know of any cases where that is true. Our studies of the top achievers in most careers and professions indicate that they "invent" ways to apply their greatest talents and existing strengths as they work. If they can't, they move on until they find a career in which they can.

These superior performers know what we hope you'll soon discover — that the secret is to find a way to maximize your greatest talents where you are right now, in whatever you are doing. If you're a full-time student, your "job" is that of a student; how do you maximize your talents in that role? If you're also a parent or work in a clothing store to pay your way through college, how do you make the most of your talents in those roles?

Because of all the rapid change in our society, half the jobs that will exist in your lifetime don't even exist yet. Therefore, college is not about preparing you for a job, or even for a career. It's about preparing you for life, to become a lifelong learner who knows how to gain the knowledge and skills that are needed for new challenges. So relax — your choice of major and even your choice of career don't lock you in for life, and you have the rest of your life to adjust the fit. There are many careers that will allow you to develop and apply a great number of strengths.

Does this mean that you can be anything you want to be when you grow up? Well, that's certainly the American dream. But it's also the American myth! It's democratic and reflects our national character to say that anyone can become the next president or CEO or movie star. But the truth is you can become only a highly developed version of who you already are — you can only grow into your own potential. You've been wired from early in life, perhaps even from birth, to love certain things, to see the world a certain way, to blossom in particular environments, and to respond naturally and easily to specific opportunities.

Just as an acorn can't become a palm tree, you can't become something other than the very best of who you already are — which is not such a bad deal after all! Reaching your full potential, becoming the person you were created to be, is an aspiration that will take a lifetime but will be much more satisfying than unsuccessfully struggling to become someone you are not.

So what is "fit" all about? Exactly what are the pieces that must fit together for a satisfying career? There are really only two of them: who you are and what you do. Psychologists call it "person-environment fit." Theologians sometimes refer to it as a "calling." We like theologian Frederick Buechner's definition of calling: "where your deep gladness meets the world's deep needs." It's all about becoming the person you were created to be in order to do the work you were designed to do. It's that simple — and that complicated.

Your Deep Gladness

It all starts with *you*. Any search for a good fit begins with a good look inside yourself. Or as Parker Palmer says, "Before I can tell my life what I want to do with it, I must listen to my life telling me who I am" (Palmer, 2000, p. 4). What is your "deep gladness"? What brings you joy? What energizes you and gets you up in the morning? These are helpful clues in your search for the right fit. We want to encourage you to see what's *right* with you. We want you to take seriously those most important and most precious parts of your identity, and then bring these aspects into the career-planning process.

If you can't think of anything that gets you up in the morning these days, reflect on when you were in fourth or fifth grade. What did you love to do? How did you spend your time? What could absorb you for hours? Psychologist Mihaly Csikszentmihalyi talks about the concept of "flow" that occurs when we enjoy a task so much that we lose all track of time and aren't thinking about ourselves or our performance.

Interestingly, adults report this experience occurs during work three times more often than in any other activity. Flow happens when you're challenged and stretched, but are equal to the task. Athletes and musicians sometimes refer to it as "playing in the zone." Everything falls into place, you don't exactly know how you did it, but you were able to excel in a way that brought deep satisfaction — that "deep gladness" we referred to earlier. People who have developed strengths and are in environments that allow their talents to flourish are far more likely to experience this "flow."

Watch any group of children and it will be clear what they love to do — and what they don't. The seeds of their future have been planted and are beginning to blossom. No one has yet told them that they can't get a job doing what they love and there's no pressure yet to follow in Mom or Dad's footsteps by becoming a doctor or lawyer. No teacher has yet said that they don't have what it takes.

There's a saying that goes, "Genius is childhood recaptured." Your childhood reflects the genius of your most naturally powerful talents. So think back to your childhood, put aside the fears that have come with growing a little older, and ask yourself, *"What would I love to do, if I didn't have to worry about making money and if I knew I could not fail?"*

Your answer is a clue to your deep gladness, and it's the most important piece of the puzzle.

After you've had a chance to think about this question, there are some other things you can do to figure out who you are and where your deep gladness lies. Talking about your Signature Themes with the most important people in your life can help; taking career inventories and discussing the results with a career counselor can give you some clues; and discussing your dreams with your advisor or your favorite professor can aid you in pinpointing what's most important to you and what you're passionate about.

Meeting the World's Deep Needs

If the first piece of the career-choice puzzle is knowing who you are and what brings you deep gladness, the second piece is connecting that to what you do — how you can meet the world's deep needs. Leaving the planet a little better off than you found it is a worthy goal. A sense of mission and purpose for your life can energize you and keep you going when you encounter the natural obstacles of life.

What kind of difference do you want to make in the world? What kind of legacy do you want to leave as your imprint after you're gone? The college years aren't usually a time when thoughts about the end of life are foremost in your mind, and that's as it should be. But the kind of life you live is being determined now by the choices you make every day. So what life are you beginning to craft for yourself? What are the first chapters of your legacy?

You've already begun to write the story that will become your life legacy. Look back over the jobs you've had, hobbies you've enjoyed, and memorable volunteer work. See any patterns? Can you put into words what you liked or disliked about each job or volunteer opportunity? On your best days, what were you doing? When you experienced a sense of fulfillment or satisfaction with work well done, what had you done to make that happen?

Some environments allow your talents to flourish more than others. Research has shown that most of the stress of life is due to the environments we're in, more so than what we are doing in those environments (Miller, 1999). Environments that reflect our values are more likely to enable us to capitalize on our talents. British author Samuel Butler said,

"People are always good company when they are doing what they really enjoy." Finding the environment that brings out your best and that allows you to develop strengths by capitalizing on your most powerful talents is the secret to making a wise career choice.

So how do you discover the kinds of environments that are likely to allow you to maximize your talents? Your previous experiences offer a clue, as does what you learn from job shadowing — following someone who is in a career you think you might enjoy over the course of several days or weeks. But there's another way.

Psychologist John Holland (1992) devised a method of determining person-environment fit back in the early 1970s when he found that there were six basic types of people and there were specific kinds of environments that seemed to fit those types. He believed that people are happiest in their work when they are in congruent environments — environments that are a good fit for them. It's important to note that people don't fit neatly into boxes like this; most of us are not only one type but are a combination, and most environments also have a mix of characteristics. But Holland's research on vocational types has stood the test of time and can be a useful lens as you think about environments that will allow you to best maximize and apply your talents. You can ask a career counselor how you take the Self-Directed Search, which is a measure of Holland's vocational types. We recommend that you take a number of different career inventories as part of your career exploration process.

A large group of college students from across the United States and the United Kingdom has taken both the Clifton StrengthsFinder and a measure of Holland's vocational types. Their responses give us some clues as to the types of environments that are a good fit for talents from certain themes. These results can be found in the appendix of this book and on the StrengthsQuest Web site. Keep in mind that each person has a unique combination of talents, so any connections between your Signature Themes and your Holland type are simply to give you a place to start as you think about meeting the world's deep needs. In the pages that follow, we've outlined some of the environments that are likely to allow your talents to flourish, based on the research we've done with the Clifton StrengthsFinder and Holland's vocational types.

It's important to remember that StrengthsFinder is not a career inventory, however, and does not tell you what career path to follow. It simply helps you discover the areas where your greatest talents lie so that you can build on them in whatever roles you're in throughout your life. Knowing more about yourself helps you in the process of figuring out the environments that are likely to bring out your best. This journey may begin in your teens, but it continues for a lifetime. Whether you are choosing a career for the first time or changing careers in midlife, the process involves knowing yourself and connecting that self-awareness to environments that will allow your talents to flourish.

Remember that strengths are developed when your greatest talents have been combined with skills and knowledge appropriate to the task. As powerful as talents are, they alone cannot allow you to experience deep gladness in your work. It's only when the talent has been honed with skills and knowledge to the point of strength that you will experience enough success to bring joy. Author Pearl S. Buck noted this when she said, "The secret of joy in work is contained in one word — excellence. To know how to do something well is to enjoy it." So the clues to the environments that might bring out your best are simply a starting place for you to consider as you begin the exploration for a connection between who you are and what you do. Gaining the skills and knowledge to do the job at the level of strength is what will allow you to achieve excellence.

The Good News

The good news is that in your talents you already have within you what you need to become your best self and achieve in several different careers. Your greatest talents are simply waiting to be discovered. It needs to be *uncovered* rather than *discovered*. That's what the Clifton StrengthsFinder helps you do: It gives you some clues that help you discover your talents. Your Signature Themes are the areas where your greatest talents most likely reside, based on how you responded to the assessment.

On the following pages, we have outlined each theme and under each have described some environments that might encourage the talents reflected in the theme. We've also provided some suggestions that will capitalize on some of the talents within that theme throughout your career-exploration process. Keep in mind that your Signature Themes combine in unique ways; the talents that lie within the Ideation theme look different when combined with the talents from the Woo, Positivity,

Communication, and Activator themes, and potentially would fit with different environments than if those talents were combined with the talents found within the Strategic, Futuristic, Intellection, and Input themes. The suggestions we give on the following pages are simply meant to provide you with a place to start exploring. They are meant to open the doors to a journey of uncovering your deep gladness and how it might meet some of the world's deep needs.

APPLYING YOUR TALENTS
IN CAREERS

Applying Achiever Talents in Careers

These observations and suggestions will help you consider careers that could best suit Achiever talents. As you think them over, select those that appeal to you most.

☐ As a talented achiever, you probably are attracted to goals. Take the time to establish clear and relevant objectives that will guide your intense efforts.

☐ Make a list of the steps to take in choosing a career, beginning with a visit to the career center on your campus. The list — and being able to cross items off it as you follow through on them — will give you a sense of direction as well as a deep sense of accomplishment.

☐ Roles that challenge you and reward your hard work will allow your Achiever talents to flourish.

☐ Work environments that provide incentives for quality or productivity are likely to bring out your best efforts.

☐ Find a place where your productivity, stamina, intensity, and drive for completion will make you a valued team member.

Applying Activator Talents in Careers

These observations and suggestions will help you consider careers that could best suit Activator talents. As you think them over, select those that appeal to you most.

☐ People with exceptional Activator talents like to jump right in and start, so your best approach to career planning is to try out various roles. Look for part-time jobs, work-study on campus, or volunteer opportunities where you can "try on" a career that looks interesting to you.

☐ Identify formal or informal leadership roles on campus where your Activator talents can flourish.

☐ Powerful Activator talents make you good at the starting line. Look for work environments that will reward you for getting people out of the blocks quickly.

☐ Consider becoming an entrepreneur. Make of list of possible businesses you could start, grow, and sell once they show a profit. Understand that you may lose interest once an enterprise is so fine-tuned to the point that it runs on its own.

☐ Understand that some supervisors and managers may feel threatened by your insistence on making decisions and acting without delay. Your Activator talents will flourish best in an environment where quick decision-making is valued and there is not a lot of hierarchical structure.

Applying Adaptability Talents in Careers

These observations and suggestions will help you consider careers that could best suit Adaptability talents. As you think them over, select those that appeal to you most.

☐ Those with great Adaptability talents often respond well to changing demands. Shadow people in careers that are attractive to you and watch how they continually respond to the varied requests of their customers or clients.

☐ Interview individuals who have jobs that demand flexibility and a comfort with rapid change. Ask what their typical day is like.

☐ Gain part-time or seasonal employment in organizations where the demand for flexibility exists hour-by-hour and day-by-day. Pay attention to ways in which your Adaptability talents benefit you in these settings.

☐ Your Adaptability talents will flourish in environments that reward responsiveness and your ability to "turn on a dime."

☐ You may thrive in chaos. Avoid environments that are highly structured or routine, with lots of rules and regulations.

☐ Talk to people in the entertainment industry. Interview designers or producers and ask them to describe their work and the types of satisfaction they receive from it.

Applying Analytical Talents in Careers

These observations and suggestions will help you consider careers that could best suit Analytical talents. As you think them over, select those that appeal to you most.

☐ Many people who are exceptionally talented in the Analytical theme are good at weighing evidence.

☐ Ask good questions of people who are currently in careers that interest you. One hallmark of Analytical talents is the quality of your questions. Put that to good use in selecting a career.

☐ Talk to people who work in such fields as accounting, finance, sciences, forensics, computer technology, journalism, or other fields that involve data analysis or problem solving to find out what they enjoy most about their work.

☐ Explore jobs that allow you to make decisions based on your evaluation of facts, data, tangible evidence, and research findings.

☐ Environments that allow you the freedom to explore and think will allow your Analytical talents to flourish.

☐ Working with data and systems analysis, engaging in research, and critiquing ideas tend to bring out your best.

Applying Arranger Talents in Careers

These observations and suggestions will help you consider careers that could best suit Arranger talents. As you think them over, select those that appeal to you most.

- ☐ People who are especially talented in the Arranger theme often arrange and rearrange bits and pieces until a pattern emerges. This talent can be useful in career planning. Map out a success plan for your education — arrange and rearrange it to accommodate all possible scenarios as you think about careers that interest you.

- ☐ Keep your options open. Explore a variety of careers, knowing that it will all fall into place at the right time.

- ☐ Environments that give you contact with people and allow you the freedom and flexibility to work with others and plan events will allow your Arranger talents to flourish.

- ☐ You may be a whiz at juggling schedules and people. Environments that call upon these talents may often be very rewarding to you.

- ☐ Your Arranger talents may be most obvious during stressful or chaotic times. Environments that encourage multitasking and are relatively unpredictable may bring out your best.

- ☐ Talk to event planners, travel agents, human resource directors, city managers, or case work supervisors. Ask them what they enjoy most about their daily work.

Applying Belief Talents in Careers

These observations and suggestions will help you consider careers that could best suit Belief talents. As you think them over, select those that appeal to you most.

☐ Spend time thinking about your "calling." Once you have articulated this mission, seek more information at the career center about careers that can help you fulfill it.

☐ A mentoring relationship can provide a valuable way for you to gain insight into the fit between who you are and what you were meant to do with your life. Mentoring and being mentored increases the chances for your behaviors, decisions, and beliefs to remain congruent.

☐ Environments that are a good fit with your own mission and beliefs will bring out your best. Seek employment in companies and organizations that exhibit a strong sense of mission — that is, a commitment to positively affecting the quality of people's lives.

☐ Research opportunities in helping professions such as medicine, law enforcement, social work, refugee relocation, teaching, ministry, and search-and-rescue. Talk with people who provide services to individuals in need. Interview those who supervise them.

☐ Environments that are people-oriented, that provide service to others, or that reward personal growth are likely to allow your Belief talents to flourish.

☐ Workplaces that respect your commitment to your family and allow for a balance between work and family demands will enable you to thrive.

Applying Command Talents in Careers

These observations and suggestions will help you consider careers that could best suit Command talents. As you think them over, select those that appeal to you most.

- ☐ Explore your career options by trying out various roles in part-time jobs or volunteer work.

- ☐ Seek to hone your Command talents by filling formal or informal leadership roles in organizations. Ask for feedback from others in the group.

- ☐ Leverage your persuasiveness when choosing a career. Talk to people in fields such as law, sales, politics, or theatre about how they use their persuasive talents to succeed.

- ☐ Investigate careers that offer upward mobility. You probably are unlikely to be intimidated by others — including people in positions considered superior to yours.

- ☐ Assume a role that permits you to create and control your own and others' work. Environments that encourage your leadership will bring out your best.

- ☐ Your comfort in "calling the shots" can be especially useful in crises. Environments that regularly deal with crises or rapid decision making will allow your Command talents to flourish.

Applying Communication Talents in Careers

These observations and suggestions will help you consider careers that could best suit Communication talents. As you think them over, select those that appeal to you most.

☐ Arrange to have conservations with people who are currently in careers that interest you. By hearing their stories, you will become better able to determine whether those environments and careers would suit your talents and interests.

☐ Go to career fairs at which you can interact with lots of different people about a great variety of roles.

☐ You might be a natural storyteller. Interview storytellers such as stand-up comedians, actors, motivational speakers, teachers, public relations specialists, politicians, ministers, and corporate trainers to see how they use their Communication talents in their daily work.

☐ Explore opportunities to serve as the spokesperson for an organization, product, political candidate, company, school district, hospital, or elected official. These opportunities would allow you to try out your Communication talents in roles that could meet some of the world's deep needs.

☐ Environments that allow for significant social interaction on a daily basis will allow your Communication talents to flourish. Steer clear of environments that do not offer this opportunity, as they might drain your energy.

☐ Cooperative, interactive, educational, and political environments are likely to bring out your best.

Applying Competition Talents in Careers

These observations and suggestions will help you consider careers that could best suit Competition talents. As you think them over, select those that appeal to you most.

☐ Explore leadership opportunities on campus, particularly in organizations where you can stimulate others to excel and win.

☐ Go to the career center and take several different career inventories, then compare yourself to others who are successful in fields that interest you.

☐ Choose work environments that challenge you and in which your success can be quantified with scores, ratings, and rankings. Avoid situations lacking meaningful, objective measurement criteria, as you often desire a "yardstick" with which you can measure your progress and compare it to that of others.

☐ Decide whether you prefer to compete as an individual or as a team member. Select employment that matches your preference either for total or shared control over final results.

☐ Environments that reward your achievement and offer status or prestige are likely to bring out your best.

☐ Talk to sales reps, politicians, lawyers, athletes, and business leaders about what they enjoy most in their work.

Applying Connectedness Talents in Careers

These observations and suggestions will help you consider careers that could best suit Connectedness talents. As you think them over, select those that appeal to you most.

☐ Use service learning opportunities on campus to explore possible careers that interest you. Spend your summers volunteering for humanitarian causes to determine the best fit for your talents.

☐ Talk to your mentor about the connections you see between your volunteer opportunities, your values, and your mission in life. This relationship can provide a valuable sounding board through which you can articulate the connections that you see so naturally.

☐ Consider dedicating a couple of years of your life to serving your country or community after graduation. Habitat for Humanity®, the Peace Corps, Volunteers in Service to America (VISTA), AmeriCorps®, GreenPeace®, and Teach for America® can be good places for you to experience a deep sense of gladness in meeting the world's deep needs.

☐ Incorporate your need to serve all of humankind into whatever career you choose. Working in fields and for organizations whose values mirror your own will enable you to feel the deep sense of meaning that is so important to you.

☐ Environments that allow you to interact with others and help them find meaning and purpose will bring out your best. Avoid environments that emphasize routine procedures or rote skills, as they may drain you.

☐ Talk to people who have made a lifetime commitment to a specific ministry within your faith tradition. Hearing them articulate their sense of connectedness and spirituality may help you determine whether this level of commitment is appropriate for you.

Applying Consistency Talents in Careers

These observations and suggestions will help you consider careers that could best suit Consistency talents. As you think them over, select those that appeal to you most.

- ☐ Interview people who are currently in jobs that interest you. Shadow them to see what they really do day in and day out.

- ☐ Go to the career center and talk with a counselor about career inventories or lists of jobs that seem consistent with your greatest talents.

- ☐ Referee intramural athletic events or help create policies in your residence hall to see if those applications of the same rules for everyone brings out your best.

- ☐ Environments that have regulations, policies, procedures, and guidelines firmly established are likely to feel more comfortable to you and enable you to be more effective and efficient. Less controlled environments probably will not be comfortable for you.

- ☐ Environments that are structured, predictable, and detail-oriented are likely to appeal to you. Search for environments where loyalty is valued and equally applied policies are the norm, as this emphasis on consistency will enable you to get more done.

- ☐ Research roles in quality assurance, risk management, safety compliance, law enforcement, and human resource analysis.

Applying Context Talents in Careers

These observations and suggestions will help you consider careers that could best suit Context talents. As you think them over, select those that appeal to you most.

☐ Talk to your mentor and to those in jobs that interest you. Ask them to tell you about their job searches. What led them to choose their particular careers?

☐ Read as much as you can about career planning, so you'll understand the process from beginning to end. That understanding of the total experience will give you the security to consider a variety of options.

☐ You recognize that past behavior is often the best predictor of future behavior. Spend some time thinking about your own past choices and how they might be connected to good possibilities for your future.

☐ Your Context talents are likely to flourish in environments that allow you to explore how things came to be the way they are.

☐ Collegial environments with strong traditions, rituals, and a sense of organizational history will often bring out your best efforts.

☐ Interview archeologists, historians, museum curators, humanities professors, or antique appraisers about their talents and what they love about their work.

Applying Deliberative Talents in Careers

These observations and suggestions will help you consider careers that could best suit Deliberative talents. As you think them over, select those that appeal to you most.

- ☐ Collect as much information as you can about the careers that interest you. Search occupational handbooks, lists in occupational guides, and online sources. Take the time to think things through, possibly listing the pros and cons of careers that interest you.

- ☐ Environments in which you can independently conduct thorough analysis are likely to help you be most effective.

- ☐ You likely are a good questioner of actions, helping others to think through their decisions before moving ahead too quickly.

- ☐ You tend to be a private person, so environments where people are known for being discreet and trustworthy will likely bring out your best. Environments that expect a lot of socializing or interpersonal interaction or that demand persuasion or selling will not be as comfortable for you.

- ☐ Explore the roles of risk analysts, financial officers, judges, and others whose work benefits from careful thinking and deliberation.

Applying Developer Talents in Careers

These observations and suggestions will help you consider careers that could best suit Developer talents. As you think them over, select those that appeal to you most.

☐ Interview people who are currently in jobs that interest you. Shadow them to see what they really do day in and day out. You enjoy having this personal connection to what interests you.

☐ Talk to your mentor about the career planning process. Use that relationship as a sounding board for making decisions.

☐ You likely have a talent for noting people's progress and for helping them become even better at what they do. Seek an environment in which your work involves getting "people done through work" rather than "work done through people."

☐ You will be most satisfied in a career that provides some type of service to people or in which organizational success is based on interpersonal relationships and your ability to help people be successful.

☐ Environments that are collaborative and people-oriented, where you can be part of a team but also have time to work one-on-one with others, is likely to allow your Developer talents to flourish.

☐ Talk to counselors, teachers, speech therapists, athletic coaches, acting coaches, life coaches, and those who work in your campus learning center to find out what they enjoy most about their work.

Applying Discipline Talents in Careers

These observations and suggestions will help you consider careers that could best suit Discipline talents. As you think them over, select those that appeal to you most.

- ☐ Collect all the information you might need about making a career choice. Use your natural discipline to organize it as you prepare to make a decision.

- ☐ Lay out all the steps of the career planning process and follow them one by one. Put the steps on a timeline, as timelines often motivate you.

- ☐ Environments in which you can maintain order for yourself and others will enable you to be most effective. Your organizational talents can be useful in a wide variety of settings.

- ☐ Environments that are structured and detail-oriented, with clearly established routines and procedures, will likely bring out your best. Cluttered, unpredictable environments may not allow your Discipline talents to flourish.

- ☐ Work that demands high levels of abstract thinking probably will not be comfortable for you. A daily routine and concrete expectations from others likely will enable you to be most productive.

- ☐ Environments that value attention to detail and commitment to accuracy will be a good fit for you. Read about the work that air traffic controllers, brain surgeons, tax specialists, and executive assistants do.

Applying Empathy Talents in Careers

These observations and suggestions will help you consider careers that could best suit Empathy talents. As you think them over, select those that appeal to you most.

☐ Talk to your mentor about the career planning process. Use that relationship as a sounding board for making decisions.

☐ Interview people who are currently in jobs that interest you. Talk to them about how they feel in those roles.

☐ Environments that provide regular social interaction and an opportunity to collaborate with others will allow your Empathy talents to flourish.

☐ The "emotional tone" of your work environment is important. You might find that surrounding yourself with others who are positive and upbeat is highly rewarding.

☐ Seek work environments in which emotions are valued and not repressed. The rich emotional economy will be the perfect environment for your Empathy talents.

☐ Interview teachers, counselors, and clergy members and ask them how they use their talents in their work.

Applying Focus Talents in Careers

These observations and suggestions will help you consider careers that could best suit Focus talents. As you think them over, select those that appeal to you most.

- ☐ Set specific goals for your career planning. What do you want to achieve by the time you graduate? This attention to your destination and how you will get there will be very engaging and will provide great benefits.

- ☐ Spend some dedicated time reading about careers that interest you and following up with internet searches. Your ability to concentrate on a task will stand you in good stead as you research career possibilities.

- ☐ Although your Focus talents can reveal themselves through highly proactive goal setting, you might sometimes need to have a target identified for you.

- ☐ You are capable of prolonged concentration and persistence, which flourishes in environments with few interruptions and little need to multi-task.

- ☐ Structured environments that are predictable, detail-oriented, and reward your dependability and follow-through are likely to bring out your best.

- ☐ You might be most satisfied in roles that have identifiable goals, purposes, and objectives, and that provide opportunities to meet your own longer-term goals.

Applying Futuristic Talents in Careers

These observations and suggestions will help you consider careers that could best suit Futuristic talents. As you think them over, select those that appeal to you most.

☐ Your ability to imagine a preferred future can be applied to the career planning process. Imagine yourself on graduation day — and five years after that. What are you doing? How did you create the opportunity?

☐ Volunteer in an organization where you can help create the future, painting vivid pictures for those who work there, helping them see the role they will take in making this vision become reality.

☐ Use the connections you establish in your jobs during college to network for the career you envision for yourself after graduation.

☐ Choose a career in which you can help others envision the future and inspire them to create it.

☐ You are capable of investing lots of time in producing original or creative works. Environments that reward vision and creativity, allowing you freedom to dream and invent, are likely to enable your Futuristic talents to flourish.

☐ Talk to architects, designers, commercial artists, city planners, and others whose careers provide the opportunity to envision the future. Ask them what they most enjoy about their work.

Applying Harmony Talents in Careers

These observations and suggestions will help you consider careers that could best suit Harmony talents. As you think them over, select those that appeal to you most.

- ☐ Talk to your mentors about the career planning process. You will value their wisdom and expertise as you make decisions.

- ☐ Interview people who are currently in jobs that interest you. Ask them what they find most rewarding about their work. Shadow them to see what they really do day in and day out.

- ☐ You work well and are helpful in team project environments. You help others work together even more productively. Your Harmony talents promote emotional stability and calmness in the group.

- ☐ Environments where consensus is the preferred strategy for decision-making and where you can work your magic behind the scenes are likely to bring out your best.

- ☐ Collaborative environments in which you can surround yourself with others dedicated to win-win solutions will allow your Harmony talents to flourish.

- ☐ Environments that lack structure or are unpredictable from day to day, or that demand high levels of creativity, are not as likely to be comfortable for you.

- ☐ Interview statisticians, tax experts, or financial planners and then compare their daily work with those in more people-oriented fields to see which sounds more agreeable to you.

Applying Ideation Talents in Careers

These observations and suggestions will help you consider careers that could best suit Ideation talents. As you think them over, select those that appeal to you most.

- ☐ Ideation talents are all about creativity. Freely imagine yourself on graduation day — and five years after that. What are you doing? How did you create the opportunity?

- ☐ Brainstorm all the possible careers that could fit your talents. Check them out online or in an occupational handbook for details, then picture yourself in each one. Which one fits best?

- ☐ Environments that reward your creativity and give you the time, space, and freedom to experiment and dream will bring out your best. Often these environments are fast-paced and freewheeling, allowing you to run your ideas past others on a daily basis.

- ☐ Avoid environments that box you in with routines or that expect precision or attention to detail. You will invest significant time and produce results without constant supervision.

- ☐ Select an organization where the leaders encourage and solicit your divergent thinking, stimulating them to consider some new approaches. You will be able to find new and better ways of doing things within the organization, and you may be of assistance in strategic planning exercises.

- ☐ Consider careers in which creativity seems to be important. Talk to strategic planners, consultants, market researchers, designers, or people in advertising to find out what they enjoy most about their work.

Applying Includer Talents in Careers

These observations and suggestions will help you consider careers that could best suit Includer talents. As you think them over, select those that appeal to you most.

- ☐ Interview people who are currently in jobs that interest you. Shadow them to see what they really do day in and day out. This personal interaction with people in careers you are considering can help you sort to the best option.

- ☐ Make the most of your willingness to include outside sources by talking to a career counselor about your interests and what you are passionate about. Talking things through with a knowledgeable counselor can give you confidence in exploring the possibilities.

- ☐ Environments where you can play a welcoming role, such as in orienting new employees or recruiting minority staff, can allow your Includer talents to flourish.

- ☐ Working with a group that is not always included by others, such as physically or mentally challenged children, will allow you to use your talents to help others feel better about themselves.

- ☐ Environments that encourage teamwork and foster social interaction and integration and will bring out your best.

- ☐ Talk to youth workers, occupational therapists, social workers, special education teachers, and missionaries to learn what they find most rewarding about their work.

Applying Individualization Talents in Careers

These observations and suggestions will help you consider careers that could best suit Individualization talents. As you think them over, select those that appeal to you most.

- ☐ You realize that there is a unique fit between who you are and what you do with your life. Go to the career center and take several career inventories. How does each one offer you a unique picture of yourself and your interests?

- ☐ Interview people who are currently in jobs that interest you. Shadow them to see what they really do day in and day out. Think about how each one responds differently to their work.

- ☐ Your talents can be useful on search committees and in recruiting processes, as you are able to see ways in which people's talents can fit particular roles.

- ☐ Careers in which you could work one-on-one with people would allow your Individualization talents to flourish, as you see each one as a distinct person and empower them to grow.

- ☐ Environments in which you can mentor others or provide feedback to individuals about their performance may bring out your best.

- ☐ Interview teachers, counselors, corporate trainers, and other individuals who are able to see the uniqueness in others. How do they use their talents in their work?

Applying Input Talents in Careers

These observations and suggestions will help you consider careers that could best suit Input talents. As you think them over, select those that appeal to you most.

- ☐ Collect as much information as you can about the careers that interest you. Go online, read books, collect all the brochures at the career center and at career fairs. The more information you gather, the better your decision will be.

- ☐ Go to the career center and take several different career inventories. What does each one tell you about your interests? What career possibilities do they suggest you to explore?

- ☐ Environments that give you the freedom to pursue threads of information and that focus on informed decision-making are likely to bring out your best.

- ☐ You probably will enjoy a career in which you are always on the cutting edge of knowledge and you can gather and share valuable pieces of relevant information.

- ☐ Choose jobs that require you to be an expert collector and consumer of research. This type of environment will energize you.

- ☐ Interview media specialists, librarians, archivists, writers, information technologists, and others who work with large amounts of information on a daily basis. What do they find most rewarding about their work?

Applying Intellection Talents in Careers

These observations and suggestions will help you consider careers that could best suit Intellection talents. As you think them over, select those that appeal to you most.

☐ Read, read, read! Gather books on careers that interest you, read biographies of people in careers that fascinate you, read all the brochures and books available at the career center. Then go online and read some more. Through your reading you will come to a better sense of clarity about the career options that fit you best.

☐ Think about the times in your life when you have felt best about your accomplishments. In your journal, write about what you did that contributed to those accomplishments and how you used your talents in each instance. Later, look for patterns in what you wrote.

☐ A work environment where you have time and space to think and reflect before responding will bring out your best. A fast-paced environment where there is pressure to sell or to follow routine procedures will not be as comfortable for you as one that allows and rewards thought and reflection.

☐ Select work in which you can share ideas and pose questions. Avoid environments where you cannot challenge the status quo or where operating procedures are completely rigid.

☐ Environments in which you can interact with colleagues and have philosophical debates will be most satisfying to you and enable you to be productive.

☐ Choose work that will challenge you intellectually. Talk to editors, theologians, or philosophy professors on campus. Ask what their work is like.

Applying Learner Talents in Careers

These observations and suggestions will help you consider careers that could best suit Learner talents. As you think them over, select those that appeal to you most.

☐ Go to the career center on your campus and take several different career inventories. What does each one tell you about your interests? What career possibilities do they suggest for you to explore? Your enjoyment of this self-discovery can motivate and guide you as you begin the career planning process.

☐ Talk to your mentors about the career planning process. Ask them how they made the decision to pursue their career. Learning about their strategies will provide you with possible tools for your own learning process.

☐ Read and study all the career possibilities that interest you. Research each one and learn what it's really like to be in those careers over a long period of time.

☐ Choose a work environment that encourages constant learning or where study is a way of life.

☐ Environments that value the learning process will bring out your best, particularly if you will have opportunities to develop strengths.

☐ Many college professors have exceptional Learner talents. Interview your favorite professors about what they find rewarding in their work.

Applying Maximizer Talents in Careers

These observations and suggestions will help you consider careers that could best suit Maximizer talents. As you think them over, select those that appeal to you most.

☐ Talk to your mentors about the career planning process. You will value their wisdom and expertise as you make decisions.

☐ Interview people who are currently among the "best of the best" in jobs that interest you. Ask them what they find most rewarding about their work. Shadow them to see what they really do day in and day out. Notice the talents, knowledge, and skills that excellence in those roles requires.

☐ You are someone for whom "talent talk" comes naturally — it's the way you see the world as you capitalize on your own and others' talents. Environments that encourage "best practices" and in which you can work collaboratively with others to continually improve the organization will allow your Maximizer talents to flourish.

☐ Choose a workplace that is known for being among the best in its field. Workplaces with lesser standards probably would frustrate you.

☐ Find work in which you can help others see their talents and how their talents make a difference.

☐ Interview business leaders and athletic or executive coaches, and ask what they find most rewarding about their work. Find out how they bring out the best in others.

Applying Positivity Talents in Careers

These observations and suggestions will help you consider careers that could best suit Positivity talents. As you think them over, select those that appeal to you most.

☐ Interview people who are currently in jobs that interest you. Shadow them to see what they really do day in and day out.

☐ Go to career fairs where you can interact with lots of different people and learn about many different roles.

☐ You will thrive in work environments that are fun, fast-paced, and people-oriented.

☐ Relaxed, social, pleasant environments where your optimism and sense of humor will be appreciated are likely to bring out your best. Avoid environments where cynicism and negativity are seen as "cool."

☐ Choose work for which you have passion. You will be energized when you are in environments that encourage your hopeful view of the future.

☐ Choose a career in which you can help others be more effective. Interview coaches, teachers, sales reps, marketing executives, realtors, or managers and ask them what they like most about their work.

Applying Relator Talents in Careers

These observations and suggestions will help you consider careers that could best suit Relator talents. As you think them over, select those that appeal to you most.

- ☐ Talk to your mentors about the career planning process. You will value their wisdom and expertise as you make decisions.

- ☐ Talk to your trusted circle of friends about how they see you. Don't ask them what career they think you should choose; instead, ask them to help you see your greatest talents.

- ☐ Careers in which in-depth, meaningful relationships are valued are likely to be most rewarding to you.

- ☐ Workplaces in which friendships are encouraged, where you can continuously learn about your clients and associates, likely will enable your Relator talents to flourish.

- ☐ Stable work environments where you can work with people you trust but also develop multiple levels of relationships probably will bring out your best.

- ☐ Interview counselors, teachers, school administrators, mediators, human resource directors, and others who help people as part of their work. Ask them about the relationships they develop and what is most rewarding about their jobs.

Applying Responsibility Talents in Careers

These observations and suggestions will help you consider careers that could best suit Responsibility talents. As you think them over, select those that appeal to you most.

☐ Make an appointment with a career counselor to talk about how to begin the career planning process. The sense of psychological ownership this step creates will engage you in the process and energize you to follow through.

☐ Interview people who are currently in jobs that interest you. Shadow them to see what they really do day in and day out.

☐ You often take the initiative, and you always follow through, so you do not need a lot of supervision. Select work in which you can be given more and more responsibility as you progressively achieve.

☐ Building trusting relationships with others is important to you, so choose environments in which you can surround yourself with dependable, trustworthy people. When selecting a team to join, be sure the others members are known for pulling their weight.

☐ Managing others could be a frustrating experience for you, as their standards of responsibility might not match your own.

☐ You will be most productive in environments where you can fully follow through on the commitments you make to others.

☐ Choose a work environment that focuses on outcomes rather than processes. Talk to law clerks, librarians, and executive assistants to see what they find rewarding about their work.

Applying Restorative Talents in Careers

These observations and suggestions will help you consider careers that could best suit Restorative talents. As you think them over, select those that appeal to you most.

☐ Search online and read all you can about careers that interest you. Take career inventories to see where your talents and interests match those who are successful in a particular field. This detailed self-analysis can get you started in a process of elimination that will clarify your career goals.

☐ Interview people who have a reputation for salvaging bad situations, turning companies around, or stepping in to solve problems no one else can seem to handle. Ask them what they enjoy about their work and what they actually do on a daily basis.

☐ Volunteer your time in an organization that needs someone to "breathe new life" into their work. This is often what you do best.

☐ Environments in which you are called upon to diagnose problems and design solutions will allow your Restorative talents to flourish.

☐ Talk to people who excel as customer service reps, surgeons, or television producers. Ask them what leads to their success and what they find rewarding about their work.

Applying Self-Assurance Talents in Careers

These observations and suggestions will help you consider careers that could best suit Self-Assurance talents. As you think them over, select those that appeal to you most.

☐ Your confidence that there is a good career fit out there for you will be an enormous asset in the career planning process.

☐ Your talents probably can give you confidence in a variety of jobs and volunteer opportunities. Try out several different roles. Which ones seem most natural to you?

☐ Workplaces and tasks that will challenge you and provide you with freedom are likely to energize you most.

☐ Environments that focus on prominent or critical projects that could intimidate others seem to bring out your best.

☐ You don't have a great need for direction or support from others, which makes you particularly effective in situations that call for independence of thought and action.

☐ Interview people in careers that involve public presentations, sales, or entertainment. Ask what they find most rewarding about their work.

Applying Significance Talents in Careers

These observations and suggestions will help you consider careers that could best suit Significance talents. As you think them over, select those that appeal to you most.

- ☐ Think about people you admire and what they have in common. Talk to them about the work they do and what they find rewarding about it. Ask them to give you feedback about your own goals and strategies for meeting them.

- ☐ Significant people do significant things. Imagine the legacy you want to leave. Picture yourself at retirement, looking back on a life that has made the world a better place. What will you have you done to accomplish that?

- ☐ Environments in which you and your significant contribution are visible to others and in which you receive recognition for a job well done are likely to bring out your best.

- ☐ Knowing you've made a significant contribution is important to you. Volunteer in organizations where you can make that difference and where your efforts will be appreciated.

- ☐ Seek opportunities to work with people you respect because they are professional, credible, and successful.

- ☐ Environments in which you are given flexibility to do things your own way are likely to bring out your best.

- ☐ Identify the specific talents that will help you make an extraordinary contribution to your workplace, and create opportunities to build on them.

Applying Strategic Talents in Careers

These observations and suggestions will help you consider careers that could best suit Strategic talents. As you think them over, select those that appeal to you most.

- ☐ Picture yourself in a career that you love. What are you doing? What path did you take to create the opportunity? Working backward from your goal is often an effective strategy for you.

- ☐ Play out a variety of scenarios in your mind to help you decide which career to explore further. List the various paths possible in your future so you can give careful thought to each one.

- ☐ Environments that are flexible and encourage creative thought and strategy will bring out your best. Opportunities to see the big picture and plan new approaches will energize you.

- ☐ Your ability to create new programs and generate multiple alternatives will be an asset to any organization you join.

- ☐ Environments that allow originality and focus more on the outcome than on specific procedures will allow your Strategic talents to flourish.

- ☐ Interview people who work in psychology, law, and consulting. Learn what they find most rewarding about their work on a daily basis.

Applying Woo Talents in Careers

These observations and suggestions will help you consider careers that could best match Woo talents. As you think them over, select those that appeal to you most.

- ☐ Introduce yourself to a great number of people in a wide variety of jobs. This broad exposure will give you a more informed idea of possible careers, and it could provide you with important career and social connections.

- ☐ Environments in which you can meet new people daily and have the opportunity to create a positive impression will bring out your best.

- ☐ Environments that value the ability to persuade or sell likely will allow your Woo talents to flourish.

- ☐ Avoid work environments in which there is little opportunity to extend your gregarious social nature.

- ☐ Talk to entertainers, corporate trainers, sales reps, attorneys, and public relations specialists to see what they enjoy most about their work.

Chapter XI

FURTHER INSIGHTS
INTO CHOOSING A CAREER

In this chapter, we want you to focus on what you've learned about your greatest talents and how you might approach the career planning process based on your Signature Themes. You've had a chance to look over the suggestions in the previous chapter. Now we'd like you to complete some exercises that will help you dig deeper. At the end of the chapter, we'll encourage you to select at least one strategy to implement immediately.

Identify the Career Implications of the Deepest Aspects of Your Identity

Ancient writers pointed to four elements that comprise the core of a person. These include heart (your deepest feelings), soul (the innermost place that contains the spark of life), mind (a variety of inner mental activities), and strength (not just physical, but all of your capabilities). Although this approach puts a slightly different twist on the concept of strengths, it offers interesting insights.

There are groups of sentence-completion statements below that reflect the deepest aspects of your personhood. Take the time to honestly and spontaneously respond to each.

Heart

1. I am passionate about _____

2. The greatest tragedy is when _____

3. I would really love to _____

Soul

1. The most meaningful thing I've ever done is _____

2. I feel a sense of destiny when _____

3. I come alive when I'm _____

Mind

1. I like to think about _____

2. I wonder why _____

3. I really believe that _____

Strength

1. I am most capable of _____

2. I have a talent for _____

3. I seem gifted in the following areas: _____

Which questions created the strongest response in you? Which ones did you leave blank? What patterns do you begin to see as you spontaneously respond to these questions? How might those responses and patterns help you in the career planning process?

Always Have at Least One Mentor, and Always be a Mentor to at Least One Person

A mentor is a person you respect for his or her wisdom and is someone from whom you are willing to learn. A mentor is a special type of advisor or counselor. He or she doesn't have to be "all-knowing" or a close friend, but should simply be willing and able to guide you in at least one helpful aspect. Often a mentor is someone who has "been there," in that he or she has done what you are interested in doing. While a mentor relationship is informal, its impact can be substantial.

Please note that we suggest having at least one mentor, but more than one is best because then you get additional perspectives.

In addition to having at least one mentor, you need to be a mentor to at least one other person. You doubtlessly have much to offer others.

You might want to start by mentoring someone who is three or more years younger than you. Mentoring does not need to be formal. Just offer friendship to someone you care about and would like to help.

Target Your Values Before You Target a Career

What do you value most? This is one of the first questions that you should consider in career planning.

Picture a target in your mind. It has five rings around a bull's-eye. The bull's-eye stands for the things that you value most.

Now, here is the challenge: Identify your six most important values, and then arrange them in order from the bull's-eye out, from your number-one (most important) value to number six.

Values Target

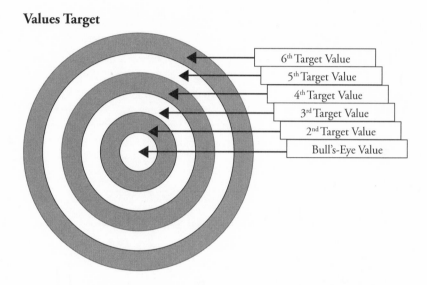

6th Target Value

5th Target Value

4th Target Value

3rd Target Value

2nd Target Value

Bull's-Eye Value

Now that you have targeted your values, remember that any career that would cause you to "miss the target" of your most important values will produce value conflicts. On the other hand, a career that helps you hit your target values produces a synergy that will likely increase your determination to achieve.

Imagine That Your Top Two Themes are Two People Who are Choosing and Planning Their Careers

This career-planning strategy will require you to use your imagination. First, consider your top two themes. If those don't resonate with you, pick the two that seem to fit you best. Next, imagine that these two themes are two people who totally embody the talents associated with those themes.

Then go back into the action items from the previous chapter (Chapter 10) and list the strategies for career exploration that fit both themes:

_____

_____

_____

_____

_____

_____

Now list the types of environments that bring out the best of the talents in these themes.

_____

_____

_____

_____

_____

_____

_____

Next, list the types of people you might interview or read about to learn how these talents are applied in their work.

_____

_____

_____

_____

_____

_____

_____

Finally, considering the strategies, environments, and people you just listed, identify ONE specific and realistic action step you can commit to taking this week as you begin the career exploration process.

This week I will _____

_____

_____

_____

_____

_____

_____

_____

Look to Your Greatest Successes for Clues to the Right Career

The whole idea of applying your greatest talents to the achievement of excellence stems from studying successful people. Extending that logic, you would be wise to study your own success patterns and then think about how your successes pertain to career planning.

To help you think about your successes, answer these three questions about your greatest triumphs:

1. What has been your most successful experience in an employment, service, or volunteer work setting?

2. What has been your most successful experience in an academic, learning, or athletic setting?

3. What has been your greatest success in an interpersonal relationship, leadership role, club, team, or organization?

After identifying your greatest success in each of those areas, focus on each success, one at a time. Relive the experience in your mind. Imagine the events and interactions surrounding your greatest successes.

As you focus on each success, ask yourself five questions.

1. What was it about that experience that makes it stand out as one of my greatest successes?

2. What did I do that contributed to producing this success?

3. What was my mental approach to this success?

4. Which talents from my Signature Themes contributed to producing this success?

5. What clues to possible careers do these experiences provide me?

Don't Plan Your Career as If It Were Some Future Event; Begin Your Career Today and Live Accordingly

You can begin to employ each and every one of these strategies today. You can immediately start acting like the career professional you want to be in the future. Today, you can put forth the attitude that you know leads to success. You can begin to develop the strengths you know you will need to apply as a professional.

If you are in school, consider it your academic career. If you have a part-time or full-time job, approach your role professionally.

Do everything you can to be a person of excellence now. It is your best preparation for future excellence.

Chapter XII

LET'S START A REVOLUTION

It's now time to travel into the future. Imagine what it would be like to live in a world in which we all knew and lived through our greatest talents. Imagine a society in which each of us would perceive others in terms of their unique talents and strengths. What would that be like? How would people feel? How would they act? What would our social systems and organizations look like? What would happen to the relationships among cultures in a strengths-based world?

Let's begin by imagining these possibilities on a personal level. Then, let's expand our thinking to include relationships, families, the world of work, organizations, and, finally, culture.

The Impact of a Strengths Revolution on You as an Individual

To consider the impact that a strengths revolution could have on you, let's start by just imagining that you are aware of all of your greatest talents. Knowing your Signature Themes alone is profound, but push your imagination to the point where you are aware of each and every one of your specific talents. Obviously, this tremendous level of self-knowledge would not come to you through one online assessment, or from reading several books, or even through an extended series of classes. This understanding would require a lifetime of learning.

However, if you were living in a society focused on strengths, people would have been helping you become aware of your unique talents all along.

To make the image of a strengths revolution more real, imagine that by age 20 you would know each of your greatest talents and have an idea of the potential for strength they offered. You would naturally have the great self-confidence that would come with awareness of your potential, and you would likely feel humility at having been given such gifts. Awareness of your talents would also bring you a sense of identity and direction.

If you were raised in a society that rigorously helped its youth fully know and understand their talents, a lot of things would change. You would be more energized to fulfill your potential. You would be less frustrated because the trial-and-error process of discovering your talents would be greatly diminished. All in all, you would be more vibrantly alive.

The Impact of a Strengths Revolution on Relationships

If everyone were aware of their own talents and those of others, we would likely place much greater value on each other and have a new basis for forming relationships in all levels of society.

Within large or small groups, entire organizations, or even couples, two things often happen when people become aware of each other's talents. First, there is increased understanding of each other. Second, people gain greater respect for each other. Can you imagine what it would be like to live in a world where everyone understood and respected each other? Phoniness, façades, and pretense would become things of the past. Authenticity would be the new norm. And of course, with more authenticity would come greater interpersonal closeness and cooperation. This would be a tremendous benefit of a strengths revolution.

The Impact of a Strengths Revolution on Families

Starting with the most basic family unit, let's think about choosing mates. If everyone knew their own talents, and if we were able to know the talents of others, we could make better decisions when selecting a mate. We would undoubtedly want to take into consideration our areas of greater and lesser talents and then look for a mate whose talents complemented our own. We would also want our own talents to complement those of our mate.

The quality of a marriage would be better if partners knew their talents and those of their mates. This knowledge would undoubtedly result in greater cooperation. If each were working from his or her talents, they could be more effective as they worked together to reach their common goals.

If a couple really understood each other's talents, roles and responsibilities could be shaped around who they each were rather than preconceived notions about gender roles. Surely, this would reduce frustration in a marriage and increase the satisfaction that the couple would experience.

By taking the strengths perspective, individuals would feel increasingly grateful for their mates, and they would realize that together, their talents could produce at even greater levels. Their intimacy would increase as they worked together.

After the strengths revolution, married couples might have a new view of their most important roles. Wouldn't it be fantastic if spouses thought that their most important responsibility was to bring out the best in each other? Love would be expressed and experienced in the nurturing of one another's talents.

Moreover, a strengths revolution would inspire parents to identify talents in their children. And maybe this would become the new standard of parenting. Indeed, families would be much healthier if everyone knew their own talents and the talents of the other family members.

The Impact of a Strengths Revolution on the World of Work

Consider what Gallup discovered in an October 2005 survey of U.S. employees: Only 31 percent were "engaged" at work, while 52 percent were "not engaged" and, most distressing, 17 percent were "actively disengaged."

Let's look at that 17 percent. These aren't just people who don't do their work well — they actively disrupt the work of others. Companies would be better off paying them to stay home. And Gallup estimates that those actively disengaged employees cost the U.S. economy approximately $300 billion per year in lost productivity.

Why are these employees disengaged? Gallup's decades of research suggest that it's because they're not in roles that match their areas of greatest potential, that they don't have productive relationships with their managers, or that their managers aren't in roles that are best suited to their talents. It is very likely that after a strengths revolution, the opposite would be true — and you would see dramatic increases in employee satisfaction, productivity, customer loyalty, and profit.

The Impact of a Strengths Revolution on Schools and Colleges

Schools and colleges typically focus on students (a) gaining the best possible education, (b) appreciating the best in art and literature, (c) developing composition skills, (d) learning important concepts and problem-solving skills in science and mathematics, and (e) developing personal qualities that promote achievement, civility, and personal well-being. We believe that after a strengths revolution, students would achieve in each of these areas at rates higher than ever before.

Of course, after a strengths revolution, a primary emphasis would be placed on helping students become aware of their talents. We imagine one-on-one sessions, group meetings, and even workshops devoted to building this awareness throughout each person's education.

Educational planning based on strengths naturally follows from building students' awareness. This planning process would help students form goals based on their talents. Even more important, strengths-oriented educational planning would continuously raise the challenge of developing strengths and inventing ways of applying great talents to increase learning and improve academic performance. Finally, students would be challenged to invent ways of applying their most natural talents in their courses of study.

We imagine that new learning paradigms may emerge as schools and colleges become focused on strengths. But the biggest change may be in the role of instructors. We can't help but ask, "What will educators need to do if they are to help students discover their greatest talents and develop strengths?"

First, they would need to know their own most powerful talents and existing strengths. Second, they would have to serve as examples. Therefore, they would have to be developing and fully applying strengths as they communicate and clarify the course content in the classes they would teach.

In addition, these educators would need to be able to identify the most powerful talents of students and encourage and assist the students in maximizing those talents through strengths development. In essence, educators would orchestrate opportunities and create activities that challenge students to apply their greatest talents as they learn.

The Impact of a Strengths Revolution on Society in General

We wonder about what would happen to ethnic and cultural divisions if everyone first knew each other in terms of their talents and strengths.

How would service organizations operate after a strengths revolution? What types of services would we need? This makes us wonder about which services are most important today.

How about faith-based organizations? What would happen to them, and what would their role be after a strengths revolution? How could they be a part of developing strengths? How would people be affected in terms of their faith and their view of God after everyone came to know, understand, and appreciate their talents?

We wonder about civic organizations, local and national governments, and international relations after a strengths revolution. Would we need as much government? Would we need as much policing? Would we need as many levels of bureaucracy if everyone knew and operated from their talents and strengths?

Finally, we wonder about elected officials. What if we really knew the talents and strengths of those who run for office? How many of those in office today would have been elected? Also consider the many talented individuals who, because of a strengths revolution, would choose to run for office or aspire to leadership roles after becoming aware of their abilities to serve the public at levels of excellence.

Again, we must admit we don't know the answers. But we are sure that the differences would be substantial, and we believe that they would be overwhelmingly positive.

The truth is, learning about talents and using them as the foundation of strengths so that you reach your maximum potential isn't good just for you; it's good for everyone. Simply put, if we all focused our lives on making the most of our talents, the world would be a better place. And could there be an outcome more worthy than that?

Now it's time to create the future. You have your work cut out for you.

Let the strengths revolution begin!

Appendix: Holland's Vocational Types and the Clifton StrengthsFinder

In the early 1970s, psychologist John Holland[1] devised a way of help-ing people make good career choices after he found that certain types of personalities were a good match for certain career environments. He found there are six basic types of people and six kinds of environments that seemed to fit those types. He believed people are happiest in their work when they are in congruent environments — environments that are a good fit for them. It's important to note that people don't fit neatly into boxes like this; most of us are not only one type but are a combination, and most environments also have a mix of characteristics. But Holland's research on vocational types stands the test of time and can be a useful lens as you think about the environments that will allow your dominant talents to flourish.

A large group of college students from across the United States and the United Kingdom has taken both the Clifton StrengthsFinder and a measure of Holland's vocational types. Their responses give us some clues as to the types of environments that might be a good fit for the talents from certain themes. Keep in mind that because each person is a unique combination of talents, these findings are simply meant to give you a place to start as you begin the career planning process.

Holland's Vocational Types

The first of Holland's types is called *Realistic*. Building things, fixing things, making things work, solving problems, and growing things bring out the best of these people. The environments that fit them best are "ac-tion oriented" — they allow for physical activity, mechanical tinkering, or being outdoors, and they don't require a lot of people skills, verbal interac-tion, or abstract thinking. Some careers that fit this vocational type are an-imal caretakers, mechanical engineers, airline pilots, correctional officers, fish and game wardens, ship engineers, firefighters, veterinary assistants, ski patrol, and forest rangers. Among our college student sample, no par-ticular theme of talents was significantly related to this vocational type.

The *Investigative* type responds best to environments that reward high academic achievement and allow these people to use their abstract thinking and scientific abilities. Opportunities to analyze information, put the pieces together, make connections, and research things bring out their best. Environments that are not highly structured and allow for freedom and independence will enable this type to flourish, because these people have the internal discipline to complete their work. They don't need supervision and they don't care to supervise others. They have confidence in their intellectual abilities and typically want to be left alone to think. Some careers that might be a good fit for this vocational type include chemists, biologists, technical writers, medical lab technicians, clinical psychologists, computer programmers, and researchers of all kinds. Among the college students we tested, the themes that were related to this vocational type were Analytical and Ideation.

The *Artistic* type prefers environments that allow creative expression. They dislike structure as much as the Investigative type does, but they are different in that their interests are more cultural and aesthetic than scientific. They are also more interested in relationships with others. So an environment that allows them to express themselves emotionally, to be creative, to be nonconforming in their behavior and dress, and that encourages their originality will be a good fit. Opportunities to create, design, write, compose, perform, and see the big picture may bring out their best, so career choices such as interior designer, artist, composer, musician, comedian, dancer, writer, actor, and musical director may result in a good fit. Among the college students we tested, the themes that were related to this vocational type were Activator, Adaptability, Command, Communication, Ideation, Input, Positivity, Self-Assurance, Strategic, and Woo.

The *Social* type tends to respond best in environments that allow them to teach or help others. Building relationships, creating trust, instructing people, resolving disputes, helping others solve problems, care giving, and healing are activities preferred by this vocational type. Environments that are relational and interactive bring out their best, allowing them to cooperate and help others grow and develop. Career choices that may be a good match might include teacher, clergy member, nurse, physical therapist, counselor, librarian, recreation director, speech therapist, athletic trainer, and social worker. The themes of Activator, Arranger, Belief, Communication, Connectedness, Developer, Empathy, Includer, Positivity, Relator, and Woo were significantly related to the Social vocational type and might be a clue that these environments are likely to allow their dominant talents to flourish.

For the *Enterprising* type, making deals, managing, persuading people, selling, starting new things, and bringing out potential are energizing activities. This type likes to work with people and ideas and enjoys leadership, speaking opportunities, and being influential. Entrepreneurial environments will bring out their best, as they are able to achieve status and be rewarded for their performance, as well as feel responsible for making things happen. Environments that are highly structured, routine, or require a lot of attention to detail will not be a good fit. Some career choices that might be a good match are lawyer, sales representative, journalist, public relations specialist, financial manager, personnel manager, athletic coach, referee, and real estate agent, as may be careers in the hospitality or travel industry. The Activator, Arranger, Command, Communication, Competition, Positivity, Self-Assurance, and Woo themes were significantly related to the Enterprising vocational type.

The final vocational type is *Conventional*. Organizing, straightening things up, getting things right, doing the numbers, and operating things tend to bring out their best. Environments that are structured and reward their loyalty and attention to detail will allow their talents to flourish. Team players who are dependable, efficient, and conscientious, as well as practical and well-organized, this type prefers to work indoors in pleasant surroundings that are predictable and run smoothly. Possible career choices include accountant, medical records technician, legal secretary, court reporter, air traffic controller, and budget analyst. In our study of college students, the Achiever, Analytical, Consistency, Discipline, Focus, Harmony, and Responsibility themes were significantly related to this vocational type.

Remember that just as your Clifton StrengthsFinder Signature Themes are not meant to define you, but rather to provide clues to your greatest talents, the Holland vocational types also are simply a helpful starting point. The insights provided by both instruments are meant to provide a beginning, rather than an end. Use them and other clues to discover your greatest talents and find environments that bring out your best. In doing so, you will create an opportunity to achieve the excellence and deep gladness that occurs when you perform at the level of strength.

1 For more information on John Holland's theory of vocational types, see his original work in Holland, J. L. (1973). *Making vocational choices: A theory of careers.* Englewood Cliffs, NJ: Prentice Hall. More recent information can be found in his 1992 book published by Psychological Assessment Resources: *Making vocational choices: A theory of vocational personalities and work environments.*

Other Technical Reports on the Clifton StrengthsFinder

The Clifton StrengthsFinder is grounded in more than three decades of studying success across a wide variety of functions in business and education and in the principles of positive psychological science. It is a Web-based talent assessment consisting of 180 item-pairs (with five response options), presented to the user over a secure connection. The item-pairs, written at a 10th grade reading level, were selected from a database of 5,000 items as informed by criterion-related validity studies (Schmidt & Rader, 1999). Each item-pair of potential self-descriptors, such as "I read instructions carefully" and "I like to jump right into things" are placed as if anchoring polar ends of a continuum. The participant is then asked to choose from that pair the statement that best describes him or her, and the extent to which that chosen option is descriptive of him or her. The participant is given 20 seconds to respond to each pair of items before the system moves on to the next item-pair. Upon completion, the respondent receives feedback including his or her top five themes and related action items.

Two reports address the psychometric characteristics (AERA/APA/NCME, 1999) of the Clifton StrengthsFinder. They are summarized below and are available, in full length, on the StrengthsQuest Web site at www.strengthsquest.com.

The Clifton StrengthsFinder Technical Report: Development and Validation (Lopez, Hodges, & Harter, 2005)

The evidence suggests that the themes are internally consistent (despite being comprised of as few as four items) and stable over periods ranging from three weeks to 17 months. Specifically, coefficient alphas range from .55 to .81 and most test-retest correlations were above .70.

The average item-total correlations and theme-score intercorrelations were examined for the entire Clifton StrengthsFinder database. Overall, the results suggest that items relate to their respective themes in a consistently positive manner. In addition, items have a higher positive relationship with their assigned themes than with other themes. The examination of the theme-score intercorrelations suggests the absence of complete redundancy among themes. This evidence lends support to the notion that each of the 34 themes provides unique information for evaluation purposes. Finally, a study correlating Clifton StrengthsFinder themes with the Big 5 constructs (McCrae et al., 2000) provided initial evidence for the measure's convergent and discriminant validity. That is, the Clifton StrengthsFinder and personality variables were not redundant and were generally associated as hypothesized.

A Technical Report of the Clifton StrengthsFinder in Relation to College Students (Schreiner, 2006)

In this study of college students from a wide variety of two- and four-year institutions in the United States and the United Kingdom, students took the Clifton StrengthsFinder, the 16PF, and the California Psychological Inventory but did not receive their results. They returned 12 weeks later and completed the CSF again. Test-retest reliability averaged .70 across the themes, with no significant gender or ethnicity differences in reliability among the students (24% of the sample were students of color).

Because only a student's top five themes are provided, we also explored the degree to which the top five themes remained the same over time. Because the Clifton StrengthsFinder contains 278,256 possible unique combinations of one's top five themes, and a change in the response to even one item on some scales can move a theme in or out of the top five, the likelihood of retaining the same top five themes is very small. However, 52% of the students in this sample had at least three themes that remained among their top five themes both times. Another 35% retained two of their top five themes over time.

Evidence of the construct validity of the Clifton StrengthsFinder was obtained in this study by correlating students' scores on each of the 34 themes with their scale scores on two personality instruments (the CPI-260 and the 16PF), since certain themes were expected to be at least moderately related to scales on these other instruments. For example, the theme of Achiever claims to measure a strong need for achievement, as well as stamina, hard work, and productivity. Thus, it ought to be related to the Achievement scales on the CPI-260 (Gough & Bradley, 1996), and in fact this was the case ($r = .47$). Woo, described as characteristic of those who enjoy the challenge of meeting new people, was expected to correlate with the Extraversion scale score on the 16PF (Cattell, 1993) and did so significantly (r = .62). In the same manner, 137 different predicted relationships between specific CSF theme scores and their counterparts on the *CPI-260* and *16PF* were explored. A total of 128 (93.4%) of these predictions were confirmed by significant correlation coefficients, providing strong evidence for the construct validity of the Clifton StrengthsFinder among college students.

References

American Educational Research Association, American Psychological Association, National Council on Measurement in Education (AERA/APA/NCME). 1999. *Standards for educational and psychological testing.* Washington, D.C.: American Educational Research Association.

Cattell, R. B. (1993). *The 16PF* fifth edition. Champagne, IL: Institute for Personality and Ability Testing, Inc.

Gough, H., & Bradley, P. (1996). *CPI^{TM} manual (3rd edition).* Palo Alto, CA: CPP, Inc.

McCrae, R. R., Costa, P. T., & Ostendorf, F., et al. (2000). Nature over nurture: Temperament, personality, and life span development. *Journal of Personality and Social Psychology,* 78: 173-86.

Schmidt, F. L., & Rader, M. (1999). Exploring the boundary conditions for interview validity: Meta-analytic validity findings for a new interview type. *Personnel Psychology,* 52: 445-464.

References and Suggested Resources

American Educational Research Association, American Psychological Association, National Council on Measurement in Education (AERA/APA/NCME). (1999). *Standards for educational and psychological testing*. Washington, DC: American Educational Research Association.

Astin, A. W. (1977). *Four critical years*. San Francisco: Jossey-Bass.

Astin, A. W. (1984). Student involvement: A developmental theory of higher education. *Journal of College Student Personnel, 25*, 297-308.

Astin, A. W. (1993). *What matters most in college: Four critical years revisited*. San Francisco: Jossey-Bass.

Buckingham, M., & Clifton, D. O. (2000). *Now, discover your strengths*. New York: Free Press.

Buckingham, M., & Coffman, C. (1997). *First, break all the rules*. New York: Free Press.

Buechner, F. (1983). *Now and then: A memoir of vocation*. San Francisco: Harper.

Cantwell, L. D. (2005). *A comparative analysis of strengths-based versus traditional teaching methods in a freshman public speaking course: Impacts on student learning and academic engagement*. Unpublished dissertation, Azusa Pacific University, Azusa, CA.

Cattell, R. B. (1993). *The 16PF fifth edition*. Champagne, IL: Institute for Personality and Ability Testing, Inc.

Clifton, D. O., & Harter, J. K. (2003). Strengths investment. In K. S. Cameron, J. E. Dutton, & R. E. Quinn (Eds.), *Positive organizational scholarship* (pp. 111-121). San Francisco: Berrett-Koehler.

Clifton, D. O. & Nelson, P. (1992). *Soar with Your Strengths*. New York: Dell Publishing.

Cope, R. G., & Hannah, W. (1975). *Revolving college doors: The causes and consequences of dropping out, stopping out and transferring.* New York: John Wiley & Sons.

Covey, S. R. (1989). *Seven habits of highly effective people.* New York: Simon & Schuster.

Cross, P. K. (1996). New lenses on learning. *About Campus, 1,* 4-9.

Csikszentmihalyi, M. (1997). *Finding flow.* New York: Basic Books.

Cushman, P. (1990). Why the self is empty. *American Psychologist, 45,* 599-611.

Dembo, M. H. (2000). *Motivation and learning strategies for college success.* Mahwah, New Jersey: Lawrence Erlbaum.

Diener, E. (2000). Subjective well-being: The science of happiness and a proposal for a national index. *American Psychologist, 55*(1), 34-43.

Doby, W. C. (1997). *UCLA's academic development plan response to the U.C. outreach taskforce report.* Unpublished manuscript, University of California at Los Angeles.

Frankl, V. E. (1959). *Man's search for meaning.* New York: Pocket Books.

Fredrickson, B. L. (2002). Positive emotions. In C. R. Snyder & S. J. Lopez (Eds.), *Handbook of positive psychology* (pp.120-134). New York: Oxford University Press.

Fromm, E. (1956). *The art of loving.* New York: Harper.

Goleman, D. (1995). *Emotional intelligence.* New York: Bantam Books.

Gottman, J. (1995). *Why marriages succeed or fail, and how you can make yours last.* New York: Simon & Schuster.

Gough, H., & Bradley, P. (1996). *CPITM manual (3rd edition).* Palo Alto, CA: CPP, Inc.

Greenleaf, R. K. (1977). *Servant leadership.* New York: Paulist Press.

Harris, M. J., & Rosenthal, R. (1986). Four factors in the mediation of teacher expectancy effects. In Robert S. Feldman (Ed.) *The social psychology of education*. New York: Cambridge University Press.

Harter, J. K., & Hodges, T. D. (2003). *Construct validity study: Strengths-Finder and the five factor model* [technical report]. Omaha, NE: The Gallup Organization.

Heath, R. (1967). *The reasonable adventurer*. Pittsburgh, PA: University of Pittsburgh Press

Hodges, T., & Clifton, D. O. (2004). Strengths-based development in practice. In P.A. Linley & S. Joseph (Eds.), *Handbook of positive psychology in practice*. Hoboken, NJ: John Wiley & Sons.

Holland, J. L. (1973). *Making vocational choices: A theory of careers*. Englewood Cliffs, NJ: Prentice Hall.

Jourard, S. M. (1963). P*ersonal adjustment: An approach through the study of health*. New York: MacMillan.

Leider, R., & Shapiro, D. (2001). *Whistle while you work: Heeding your life's calling*. San Francisco: Berrett-Koehler Publishers.

Leonard, G. (1991). *Mastery: Keys to success and long-term fulfillment*. New York: Penguin Books.

Light, R. J. (2001). *Making the most of college: Students speak their minds*. Cambridge, MA: Harvard University Press.

Lopez, S. J., Hodges, T., & Harter, J. (2005). *Clifton StrengthsFinder technical report: Development and validation*. Princeton, NJ: The Gallup Organization.

McClellan, D. C. & Steele, R.S. (1973). *Human motivation: A book of readings*. Moonstown, New Jersey: General Learning Press.

Miller, A. F., Jr., & Hendricks, W. (1999). *Why you can't be anything you want to be*. Grand Rapids: Zondervan.

Notarius, C., & Markman, H. (1993). *We can work it out: Making sense of marital conflict*. New York: Putnam.

Pace, R. C. (1979). *Measuring quality of effort.* Los Angeles: UCLA Laboratory for Research on Higher Education.

Palmer, P. (2000). *Let your life speak: Listening for the voice of vocation.* San Francisco: Jossey-Bass.

Palmer, P. (1998). *The courage to teach.* San Francisco: Jossey-Bass.

Pittenger, D. J. (2005). Cautionary comments regarding the Myers-Briggs Type Indicator. *Consulting Psychology Journal: Practice and Research, 57*(3), 210-221.

Powell, J. (1970). *Why am I afraid to tell you who I am?* Allen, Texas: Tabor Publishing.

Rath, T. (2006). *Vital friends: The people you can't afford to live without.* Princeton, NJ: The Gallup Press.

Rosenthal, R., & Jacobson, L. (1968). *Pygmalion in the classroom: Teacher expectations and pupils' intellectual development.* New York: Holt, Rinehart & Winston.

Schmidt, F. L., & Rader, M. (1999). Exploring the boundary conditions for interview validity: Meta-analytical validity findings for a new interview type. *Personnel Psychology, 52,* 445-464.

Schreiner, L. (2004). [Results of a strengths-based approach to the first-year seminar at Azusa Pacific University.] Unpublished raw data.

Seligman, M. E. P., & Csikszentmihalyi, M. (2000). Positive psychology: An introduction. *American Psychologist, 55*(1), 5-14.

Senge, P. M. (1990). *The fifth discipline.* New York: Doubleday.

Sireci, S. G. (2001). Standard setting using cluster analysis. In C. J. Cizek (Ed.), *Standard setting: Concepts, methods, and perspectives* (pp. 339-354). Mahwah, NJ: Lawrence Erlbaum.

Snyder, C. R. (1994). *The psychology of hope: You can get there from here.* New York: The Free Press.

Snyder, C. R., & Lopez, S. J. (2006). *Positive psychology.* Thousand Oaks, CA: Sage.

Steele, C. M. (1997). A threat in the air: How stereotypes shape intellectual identity and performance, *American Psychologist, 52,* 613-629.

Stipek, D. (1998). *Motivation to learn: From theory to practice.* Boston: Allyn & Bacon.

Strug, K. & Brown, G. (1996) *Heart of gold.* Dallas, Texas: Taylor Publishing.

Tinto, V. (1987). *Leaving college.* Chicago: University of Chicago Press.

Trent, J. W., & Medsker, L.L. (1968). *Beyond high school.* San Francisco: Jossey-Bass.

Trent, J. W. (1970). *The decision to go to college.* Washington D.C.: U.S. Department of Health, Education and Welfare.

Acknowledgments

If "it takes a village" to raise a child, it could be said that it took a village or even a city to develop the StrengthsQuest program. If this work resonates with you, many people will grow from your gratitude. We will mention a few.

A broad base of people contributed to the creation of the Clifton StrengthsFinder. Thousands of individuals who were judged to be successful provided interview responses from which the descriptor items were created. Hundreds of UCLA students and Gallup interviewers contributed ideas, responded to trial questions, and gave meaningful feedback.

Tom Rath, as StrengthsQuest Program Leader, along with Piotrek Juszkiewicz, the Project Manager, provided the organization, technical know-how, and inspiration to keep the entire program moving ahead day by day. Mark Pogue kept the needs of the market clearly in mind.

A gifted technical team put it all together. Jeff Briggs and Bret Bickel led a group of dedicated technologists in building the StrengthsQuest Web site. These invaluable people include: Jon Conradt, Sol Espinosa, Swapan Golla, Jeya Govindarajan, Pohl Longsine, Jesse McConnell, Christopher Purdy, Vishal Santoshi, Sam Snyder, and Collin Stork.

Editors Geoff Brewer and Paul Petters streamlined the content, with help from Kelly Henry, Drs. Maribel Cruz, Christy Hammer, Joe Streur, and Rosemary Travis, Gallup Senior Analysts, not only added insights to the text, but also checked its applicability. Dr. Phil Stone, a professor of psychology at Harvard University, and Dr. Lee Noel, founder of Noel Levitz, sharpened both the text and the goals. Kim Simeon produced the attractive and easy-to-read layout.

Pam Ruhlman and Jules Clement have tended the collection and organization of the StrengthsFinder assessments, which have already exceeded 400,000. Thanks also go to 40% of the 400,000, who have shared their Signature Themes with their friends.

We owe a special debt to Michael Anderson and his wife, Rochelle, who solidified our determination by demonstrating the growth in confidence that came from understanding their strengths.

Irma Anderson typed the original manuscript thoughtfully and with care. Without her daily determination and enthusiasm to produce a useful book, it probably would not have happened.

Special thanks go to Dr. Stephanie Juillerat for her encouragement and insights during the revision process and to Dr. Karen Longman for her feedback on the revised and new material.

Finally, we must express our gratitude for the powerful energy created by thousands of people across the country who reported great experiences after learning about their great talents, and who declared their desires to be a part of this revolutionary strengths movement.

—Don, Chip, and Laurie

*Editor's note: As mentioned above, more than 400,000 people had taken the Clifton StrengthsFinder assessment prior to the initial release of this book in 2002. Today, as we release the second edition, that total has climbed to more than **two million** people.*

Gallup Press exists to educate and inform the people who govern, manage, teach, and lead the world's six billion citizens. Each book meets The Gallup Organization's requirements of integrity, trust, and independence and is based on Gallup-approved science and research.